GARDENING WITH WATER, PLANTINGS AND STONE

Carroll Calkins

GARDENING WITH WATER, PLANTINGS AND STONE

Illustrated by
MAURICE WRANGELL

WALKER AND COMPANY ✳ NEW YORK

PHOTOGRAPHERS

Ralph Bailey   14, 25, 41, 73, 89
James Brett   83
Gottlieb Hampfler   p. vi, vii
Kent Oppenheimer   114, 119
Theodore Osmundson   p. ii, 142, 143, 148
Gottscho-Schleisner   p. viii, 8, 23, 33, 63, 79, 84, 96, 99, 107, 110,
    122, 135, 139
All others by the author

First published in the United States of America
in 1974 by the Walker Publishing Company, Inc.

Published simultaneously in Canada
by Fitzhenry & Whiteside, Limited, Toronto.

Contents

GARDENING WITH WATER, PLANTINGS AND STONE

*The flow of water need
not be large when the
stonework and plantings
are well selected and
arranged. Ferns, wisteria
and pine are used
effectively here.*

Part I

THE WONDER OF WATER

There's nothing to compare to it. It splashes, gurgles, sings and roars. It runs swiftly, stands still, rises gently—as the morning mist—and crashes down with the thunderous power of Niagara.

Droplets catch the sun and make a rainbow. The surface reflects the sky and tells the vagrant story of the wind. Ever-yielding, so it seems, it has a force that surpasses understanding. Persistent as the ages, it carves mountains into canyons, wears stone to sand and works its way through anything that man has ever known.

Water is an elemental source of life and beauty. There are lilies and lotus and other lovely plants that grow only with their roots submerged. There are ferns, sedges, reeds and mosses that grow only at its edge.

There are many ways to use pools and ponds, rivulets and rills, puddles, sprays and falls to bring more pleasure to daily life.

It is the purpose of the following pages to help you do just that.

Right: Calm, cool corner in a formal setting. Low-growing roses are used to soften the edges of the cut stone coping.

Below: Man-made meandering stream brings movement and bright reflections to a quiet country garden.

1

Consider What It Can Do for You

The most important of the dozens of good reasons for adding an accent of water in your garden is the pure pleasure it can give in its myriad forms, as mentioned on the foregoing page. This beauty and appeal have always been recognized. For as long as plants and flowers have been grown for pleasure, water has been on the scene. It played a major role in the gardens of the Moors, the Egyptians and the Chinese who first turned their hands to developing beauty out of doors and created gardens as we know them today. The Japanese made an art of using water, particularly in small amounts and in a small space.

The ancient purpose still applies. But today there are new and even more compelling reasons for using water in your garden. As land becomes more expensive and the space around our houses becomes smaller, and as air pollution and the noise we hear on all sides become more of a problem, water in the garden takes on a new note of importance.

In terms of making the most of the space you have, almost nothing else that you can add to your garden will give as much pleasure as water—in so small an area. By simply dripping water down an existing wall of brick or stone, you can give the wall a totally new and different character, and no usable space is appropriated. The most elegant of wall fountains project out from the wall only a foot or so, and the useful space they take up is negligible. Even a small cascade set in a corner can catch the sunlight and add the gentle music of falling water to the garden scene and takes up very little land.

A phenomenon known in every household was the title of a Broadway play called *You Know I Can't Hear You When the Water is Running*. Well, it works the same way in the garden. The sound of running water is pleasant and predictable and can serve beautifully to screen out traffic noise and other unwanted sounds. A fine example of this is Paley Park in New York City. On 53rd Street, in midtown Manhattan, which is hardly an oasis of quiet, there is a little park that seems marvelously tranquil and still. It seems quiet because there is a high wall of water cascading vertically down over rounded rocks set in the concrete wall. This is the sound you hear and enjoy, and it effectively screens out the racket of the traffic streaming by on the street. The size of the problem, and the solution, in Manhattan are much larger than you will have in your garden, but the principle is the same. You can use water as aural camouflage to screen out some of the unwanted noise.

While the amount of air cleaning a vertical jet of water can actually accomplish is questionable, there's no doubt that it can make the air seem cooler and more pure and refreshing. A series of tall narrow jets of water on the windward edge of a sitting area can have a definite cooling effect. The splash of the water is also a psychological cooler, probably because it summons up thoughts of a mountain stream or waterfall.

The wise use of water can also be considered a factor in the constant battle to reduce the amount of weekly garden maintenance.

Whether you realize it or not, every inch of the land that's under your control must be maintained in one way or another. Flowers must be planted after the beds are made ready. Lawns must be mowed, watered, fertilized and otherwise cared for. Shrubs and trees must be pruned. Brick and concrete must be swept, and the edges often must be trimmed. The leaves must be raked, and the list goes on. This is not all bad, of course. These routine productive chores provide much of the pleasure of gardening. But of the time you set aside for garden work, a well-designed water feature, properly installed, will require relatively little upkeep in comparison to the pleasure it can give.

The installation is also easier than it has ever been before. Anyone can learn to work with the new plastic pipe and fittings. The skills of a plumber and the tools for cutting, threading and fitting metal are no longer required for small pools in the garden. Submersible electric pumps make it easy to recirculate the water for small fountains and cascades. There are ready-made underwater lights that anyone can install safely and inexpensively. There are also tough plastic materials in sheet form with which you can easily line a hole dug in the ground to make a small pool that will last for years.

Basic instruction and sources for these easy-to-use materials are given later in the book.

Originally narrow with overgrown banks, this stream was widened, and a waterfall built, to make it more rewarding.

2

Getting Off to a Good Start

The choices are overwhelming in their variety. Should you have a formal pool, a small woodland pond, a reflecting pool, a fountain, a fall or a stream? The sheer matter of choice keeps many gardeners from going any further than a few pleasant thoughts about how nice it would be to have something in the way of a water feature around the house.

With this subject, as with all aspects of the landscape, a good design starts with a thorough understanding of the immediate environment, which calls for a hard, fresh look at all the land you have. The survey should be slow and systematic. Chances are you have never really looked hard at every. inch of your land seeking opportunities to provide for more beauty and pleasure by the addition of water in any possible form.

The proper attitude for this exercise is a determination to find ways to use water to your advantage. At this early stage don't even think about the cost, or the time it might take. Don't think in terms of practicality or maintenance. Think now only of possible opportunities to exploit the wondrous ways of this amazingly adaptable element called water.

Before you start your tour, preferably on a leisurely warm and sunny morning, think back upon the ways you have enjoyed seeing and feeling and hearing water in its natural settings.

Your garden is, in its way, a natural setting, and you will be creating a microcosm of a natural scene. And you will, by the way, discover many other things about your landscape on this tour. You may even find that adding water is not the first thing you should do. It may well become second or third on the list.

Start at the street in front of your house and think about guests arriving by car. Where do they park? How do they get to the front door? How clearly marked is their route, and how inviting? Could an added water feature provide more beauty and interest here?

If there is a shapely small tree beside the walkway to the door, a mirror-like area of water near its base could reflect the form of the branches. Not only the shape but the color of the blossoms or fall foliage will be picked up in this bright spot.

A pool of this kind should usually be small and simple. It may be small enough to be picked up and rinsed out because it will catch fallen blossoms, seed pods, twigs and leaves in the course of the season. To position it properly and get the size right, you can experiment with a wood frame made of 2 by 2's and a sheet of heavy black plastic—for better reflection. Then you can adjust this liquid mirror so that it will reflect exactly the part of the tree you want to see from the path. The principle to remember is that the angle of reflection equals the angle of incidence.

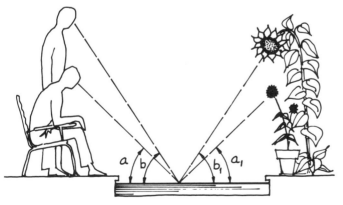

$$a = a_1; \quad b = b_1$$

Position the water, or the objects you want to see reflected, in accordance with the necessary "angle of incidence."

If there's a turn in the walk, you will notice that this slows you down as you approach and you automatically look down to check your footing. This point, either on the inside or the outside of the walk, could be an effective place for a shallow pool of interesting shape or texture or even a flat bed of river-washed rocks kept glistening wet with a small spray. The Japanese are very adept at catching the eye with small delights where there is a change in the direction of a path or bridge.

Right here is where you might want to make some other improvements before you add a water feature. If the route to the house from the drive is not clearly marked and if the walk is not interesting, you might want to concentrate on this first and add the water later. If you like the idea of a reflection to double the impact of a tree when it is in bloom, it may first be necessary for you to plant a tree in the appropriate spot.

Water is a magnificent mirror that can more than double the effect of a beautiful setting.

If you have a front entry or porch of sufficient size to accommodate a small container of water, with perhaps some floating aquatic plants in it, you may want to try that idea. Guests stand and

look around while waiting for someone to come to the door. It is an act of hospitality to give them something of interest to enjoy. Whatever you do might well be combined with a night light, which is also needed for safety, pleasure and comfort at an entryway.

The Side Yard

If you live on a city or suburban street, the side yard, that space between your house and your property line, is probably narrow and the opportunities for using water or any other decorative feature are limited. In some cases, however, a window looks out on the side yard, and a decorative feature, which could include water, would improve the outlook. If there is a wall or fence along the side boundary, a wall fountain would work beautifully nearby. In Part I, Chapter 5 you will find some interesting ideas for displaying water on a vertical surface.

The Space Behind the House

The back yard or garden offers the most opportunity for pools and fountains. This is where the space is and where most families enjoy whatever outdoor living they have arranged for.

Let's say that a back door, perhaps from the kitchen, opens to this area. Every time you go outside you go through this door. And what do you see? Step outside and look around. What do you see if you look straight ahead, and then slowly to the right and to the left? What would you rather see? How about a clump of small trees to block that view of the neighbors' yard, or a single spreading tree to screen the view of a telephone pole? Are there existing plantings that should be made larger or trimmed back to create a more pleasing outlook?

Remember that you look at this view every time you go outside. If you find you have not really been seeing it, that may well be because it is not very attractive.

This may seem to have nothing to do with

water, but adding a water feature will not help much unless the basic structure of the landscape is reasonably sound. If you don't have a good solid footing when you step into the yard (a patio or terrace or other paved area that will serve for sitting and eating and entertaining outdoors), it may be too soon to be thinking about the exquisite refinements of a water garden. The refinements and decorative features can wait until the areas involved have been made to fulfill whatever their primary function may be.

The primary function of a front garden is to provide an attractive front to the public. The entry, from the driveway to the front door, is to help people get comfortably and safely in and out of the house.

The side yard is essentially for circulation to make it easy to walk from front to back and to get wheelbarrows and other necessary tools and equipment from the back to the front yard.

The back yard can be whatever you want it to be and can afford. It may be a place for young children to play—with supervision. It may be a place for older children to have a tree house or clubhouse or hideaway in a far corner. This may be a tent or a packing case, but there is a time in the life of a child when this private place (not too far from the kitchen) is terribly important.

This is the classic place for a terrace or patio large enough for family dining and for entertaining. This is where the fruit trees will probably grow—if there is enough space. The vegetable garden, the compost pile and the dog house may all be competing for this space.

If you are a hobby gardener, there will be roses or rhododendrons or bulbs, beds of annuals or a perennial border here.

Some of these pleasures and conveniences are what you should be dreaming of as you stand at the back door and survey your private domain.

3

You're Lucky
if the Water
Is Already There

Lucky, yes. But your hand is forced. You will have a water garden whether you want it or not. And there will be work to do. You may have a stream, a pond of some kind or a low spot where water stands for part of the year. In any event there are ways to capitalize on these situations. They can be dramatized and made to do more for you.

No matter what the size, there are a few principles of improvement and development that can apply. The width, the depth and the direction can be controlled. The rate of flow, however, depends on the vagaries of nature—in terms of rainfall—and the slope of the land.

It might be well to point out here that there are varying points of view as to what constitutes "improvement." In the terminology of the U.S. Army Engineers and other efficiency-oriented developers, to improve a stream means straightening it and lining the sides and bottom with stone and concrete so that the water moves along as quickly and quietly as possible. Such an attitude may be a welcome one in case of a flash flood, but it is not the gardener's point of view. Suffice it to say that, if a tract builder says that a waterway could be "improved," he may not mean what you think he does.

The first consideration is the direction the water goes—the route it takes across your land. The

Improving a Stream

point is to put the water where you want it, where you can see it, where you can enjoy it. You cannot make it go uphill but in almost any other direction the flow can be changed. You can bring the water close to a sitting area or to a place more readily in view through a window in the house. The theory of moving a stream bed is simple. The actual doing can range from the merely difficult to backbreaking.

It pays to make sure you know where you want the stream to go before you start the work of moving it. You can lay out two roughly parallel lengths of heavy twine or light rope to mark the direction and width of the new stream bed, and it can be easily moved until you get it the way you want it. When you think you have it right, it's a good idea to dig a shallow, V-shaped trench along both new banks of the stream and study them for a few days from every angle of view and decide whether or not any adjustments will be required. Once you are sure you will have what you want, you can take the shovel firmly in hand and start to dig.

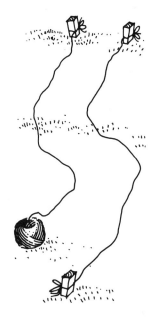

It pays to establish the path of a stream before you start to dig it out.

The soil you remove should be piled beside the original stream bed so the flow of water is diverted to the new bed and the soil will be at hand to use for fill.

When the direction has been decided upon, then it can be checked to be sure that the slope really is downhill. It is not easy to judge the slope of rough ground with the eye alone. An easy way to get the first reading is to use a length of garden hose. Lay it along the middle of the stream bed as plotted and pour water through a funnel into the uphill end. If it runs freely out the other end, the slope is sufficient to move the stream along.

The next step is to dig a narrow trench along one edge of the new stream bed and divert a part of the existing stream into it. Or you can fill it with water through a hose to see how it runs. If the rate of flow suits you, it is safe to go ahead and excavate the full width. This narrow "pilot stream" will also help you to determine whether there is enough drop in the run to establish a riffle or waterfall.

If there is enough slope in the run of the stream to make a waterfall, it will be worth the effort to do so for the sake of the sound alone. The longer the drop, the more potential for sound.

Sometimes water running over rocks set on a steep slope to make a riffle will produce more sound than on a straight drop of the same distance. If the drop is straight, a flat rock set just above the surface at the bottom of the fall will usually cause more splash than if the water falls directly into the bottom pool. The splashing water creates a spray and on a sunny day the droplets can catch the light and glisten like crystal.

Unfortunately there is no way to tell in advance what the sound will be, so simply experiment with various alignments of the rock to get the most sound you can. It is a delicate tuning process and takes considerable patience, but it is worth while.

If the flow in the season of high precipitation may create flooding, lay the rock up without mortar. Then, when the water is too high and flows too fast, the top rocks will wash out and the stream is more likely to stay within its banks than to flood the surrounding area. This is a very primitive sort of flood control, and the dam will have to be rebuilt when the high-water season is over. It can, however, prevent some flooding and may be advisable.

If some flooding is predictible, it will pay to do some preparation in advance. Study the lay of the land to see if a wide, shallow depression just beyond the banks of the stream could be created to handle some runoff. If well-rooted turf can be established between floods, the water will simply

How to Tune a Stream

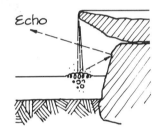

The quality of the sound of splashing water can be controlled somewhat by creating an echo chamber behind the fall.

overflow into this area and not tear up the soil. A wide, meadow-like, grassy area adjacent to a stream, where practicable, will also take some of the pressure off the banks when the water is high.

Think of the water as a force that must be expended, and do what you can to let it expend itself with as little damage as possible. Keep the overflow area streamlined because any obstruction will create turbulence that may break through the surface cover. Once the surface is broken, the force of the water will tend to strip it away—no matter what it is. Of course, if you go all out and make a dam with an adjustable spillway, you can readily control the flow.

Cutaway section shows how the water level can be controlled by setting boards in a concrete form with notches at the end to receive them. By removing all the boards the silt that will accumulate behind the dam can be flushed downstream.

Some tips on working with rock: Pick out good flat rocks and lay them out so the largest can go on the bottom before you start building. Put the heavy pieces on the bottom and fill the chinks as you go—with moss, grass and smaller rocks. To make a really watertight dam, line the back side with heavy polyethelene sheeting.

If grass grows right up to the edge of the stream, the roots will help protect the bank from erosion. If the stream is fairly straight, not too fast-running, and of even temperament, the banks will stabilize themselves. Erosion begins when the rate of flow is dramatically increased and especially on the curves of a stream. When the bank turns, the water sluices into it and tends to wash it away. A stream always works to straighten itself out. Watch for these stress points and line the bank with rock the flat sides out. If you don't carry the top line of the facing rock much above the level of the water, the lined effect will not be unattractive.

In some cases a stream can be widened, usually on the outside edge of a curve, to make a small pond. A larger pond can be made behind a dam. Making a pond too wide is a waste of time and effort, because the stream will find its own dimensions and the edges of the area you have laboriously dug out will silt up and must be continually dug out again. In a few seasons of flooding and drought you will find out how wide an area can be maintained without requiring too much hard spade work.

After a few seasons of working with a shovel to establish the desired contours, you may find that the ways of nature are after all the most aesthetic.

The shapes that are made by water current, and the transitions from the plants that grow along the edge to the sand or gravel under the water of the stream, are among nature's minor masterpieces. To see and savor their ever-changing subtlety is

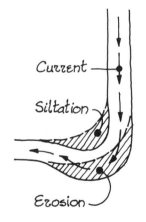

In its natural inclination to flow in a straight line, water cuts away the outside of a bend in a river or stream bed and deposits silt on the inside as shown here.

one of the constant joys of having a stream or pond on your land.

A large rock, or a grouping of large rocks, can be used to make an island if the stream is wide enough to accommodate it. This will establish a sculptural form in the water (which can be doubled in size by its reflection) and will create interesting new patterns of waves and currents.

The Japanese, who have had centuries to consider the matter in their gardens, seem to have found that a group of three, five or seven rocks is easiest to arrange into a pleasing design.

Improving a Pond

If you have a country place, you may be fortunate enough to have a pond, or a low area that can be developed into one. A full-fledged, well-developed pond is a marvel of ecological relationships. The necessarily elegant and precarious balance of accumulated water, soil (mud), plants, fish, frogs, algae and other microcosms is something to strive for, but can be obtained only under ideal conditions.

Let us consider, for inspiration, some thoughts on a natural pond by Henry Thoreau whose fascination with Walden Pond in Massachusetts is well recorded in his writings.

A Bog Is Not Necessarily Bad

If your goal is a nice green lawn, or a flower bed in the corner of the garden, that low spot where water always seems to gather will be a source of trouble.

If flowers or vegetables are what you want to grow, the soil must be reasonably light and very well drained.

But with a shift in your gardening point of view a boggy low spot can become an interesting accent in the landscape—providing, of course, that it is in a location that would relate such a feature to the rest of the garden in an attractive way.

If the low boggy area is too small, or happens

Walden Pond photographed in 1908.

". . . . *A lake is the landscape's most beautiful and expressive feature. It is the earth's eye; looking into which the beholder measures the depth of his own nature. . . . It is a mirror which no stone can crack, whose quicksilver will never wear off, whose guilding Nature continually repairs; no storms, no dust, can dim its surface ever fresh;—a mirror in which all impurity presented to it sinks, swept and dusted by the sun's hazy brush,—this is the light dust-cloth—which retains no breath which is breathed on it, but sends its own to float as clouds high above the surface, and be reflected in its bosom still.*

—HENRY DAVID THOREAU, *Walden*

to be an uninteresting shape, it can be dug out to suit your needs and preference. The area is obviously a catch basin for runoff, or for rising underground water. Chances are that the area can be enlarged somewhat without danger of its going dry. It is safer to widen than to deepen it because, in deepening it, there is the possibility of breaking through the clay formation and losing some of the water to the subsoil below.

To enlarge a boggy place, the land can in some cases be reshaped so that more surface water moves to that area. Another possibility is to lay underground tile from a downspout and bring the water from a roof. If the supply is to be unpredictably variable, as it will be from a downspout, there should be an overflow to keep the level of water right for the plants you have chosen for the bog.

You may want to establish an edge to mark the end of the lawn area clearly if it happens to be surrounded with grass. Or you may prefer to let the vegetation in the bog merge gradually with the surrounding land. The bog plants you choose will do this automatically. They will grow well where there is constant moisture at the roots and less well as the soil gets drier.

If the area is more than 3 or 4 feet in diameter, there should be a few steppingstones firmly placed to provide access for planting and maintenance, and to walk on so one can enjoy the small biological marvels that develop and grow in a boggy place. Steppingstones may be natural ones, but it is not easy to find them of the right size and shape—particularly within carrying distance. A little shopping in a masonry yard may turn up something to your liking. There are solid blocks used for foundations, and round covers for septic tanks that will work in various situations.

To determine how large the pieces should be, probe with the blunt end of a baseball bat to see how deep you must go to reach a density of material that will support the steppingstones you get.

Steppingstones can be as much a feature of design as a convenience in walking into a boggy place for cleaning and maintenance.

The candelabra primulas (P. japonica) *can be combined beautifully with ferns in moist soil. A planting of rhododendron provides a handsome year-round green background.*

4

What It Takes to Start From Scratch

To create a "natural" pond from the bare earth is a considerable undertaking and success can never be guaranteed. Unless certain definite requirements are readily at hand, you would be well advised not to try.

There must be a supply of water that is dependably constant. This can be from a pump if you are blessed with enough flow from a well to supply it. It may be a stream or spring. It may also come from the skies in the form of rain or snow and flow then to a place where it can be retained.

If the pond is filled by nature, it will look at home in its setting. It must naturally be in a hollow place where water will collect. This is not to say that it must be at the very bottom of your property. It can also be on a hillside but in a hollow in the slope.

If you have a supply of water and plan to dig a pond, you could conceivably put it anywhere. In the process, however, you might violate the lay of the land and put the pond where it would obviously never appear in nature. Man-made "natural" ponds must be thoughtfully sited to have a natural appearance. If this is not possible, it may be best to make an obviously man-made pond using concrete for the bottom and sides.

The size will depend on the site and the water supply. The shape should reflect the shape of the surrounding hollow. If you are serious about a project of this scope, seek out as many natural ponds as you can and get a feel for the outline of the body of water in relation to the surrounding land. Photographs of the pond from various angles can be helpful in determining the shape and in laying out the surrounding plantings.

While personal preferences and aesthetic considerations are important in siting a pond, the practical fact of the matter is that a successful pond can be established only where the subsoil has enough clay content to hold water.

Naturally wet and boggy areas are the logical places to look for this condition, but the only sure way to determine the true nature of the subsoil is to dig down to where the bottom of the pond will be and examine the soil. If you want a pond 10 feet deep, a 6-foot test hole will not give you a true indication of the makeup of the bottom.

Such a job is not for a man with a shovel. The test hole should be large enough to give a sampling of the area. Digging an area 6 to 10 feet in diameter is obviously a job for a back-hoe. When the hole is dug, carefully examine the material at the bottom. If it is loose and sandy or gravelly, it won't hold water unless there is a good layer of clay just below. If the bottom is heavy and sticky clay, the chances are that it will hold water. In any event, fill the hole and see what happens.

The U.S. Department of Agriculture has advisors (called District Conservationists) who can be of great help to anyone with a piece of land in the country. You can find your local advisor's number in the telephone book under United States Government, Agriculture, Department of. The advisor can readily analyze the soil in the bottom of the test hole and tell you how well it may or may not hold water. If the contractor who does the job of back-hoeing has had experience in digging ponds, he, too, can give advice as to where to dig, and he will be knowledgeable about the water-holding capacity of the hole he digs.

If the test hole stays filled well enough for you to go ahead with the pond, a bulldozer will be required for the job. The size of the pond, and thus the size of the bulldozer and the cost of the digging, will depend on its eventual use. You may want the pond for swimming, boating, fishing or simply for the decorative effect of a mirror of water set into a rough piece of land.

If the pool is for swimming, it is best to have it 12 to 14 feet deep so that it will be deep enough for diving even if the water level drops a few feet, as it is likely to do in midsummer.

Outline the area roughly with stakes—and roughly is the word—for a bulldozer is not a precision instrument. Keep in mind that a pond is more interesting if some areas of the bank are steep and others slope gently to make a beach area. If you wish to attract small birds to the water, there must be some very shallow areas, no more than 2 or 3 inches deep, around the edge.

If large rocks are available, a few of these set at random around the edge of the pond—in and out of the water—make a pleasant accent. If there are trees you want to save, keep the digging machines well away from the root area. Remember that roots extend well beyond the perimeter of the foliage. Soil should not be piled over the root area, or scraped away from the top, as either operation can damage or kill a tree.

Keep trees far enough from the pond so the roots will not break through the underwater surface and cause leakage. All the marking and planning should be done before the bulldozer arrives. In addition to deciding the site, size and shape of the pond, you must decide where the spillway will be. Its height, of course, establishes the water level when the pond is full. Its location will determine where the overflow goes. The overflow may be considerable when there are heavy

With just three rocks and a plant, a major point of interest can be created at the edge of the water.

rains and the water must be directed to areas where no harm will be done. Water will find the course of least resistance. With this fact in mind you should plan to keep it from doing any damage. The soil scooped up from the hole can be used to create a levee where required to retain the water.

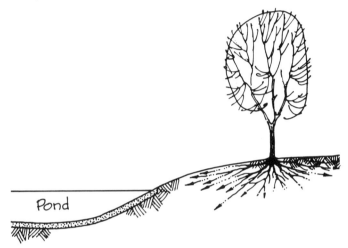

Trees should be set far enough from the pond so the roots will not break through the clay bottom.

One rather sophisticated solution to controlling the overflow of a farm pond in upper New York State is a stand-pipe connected to a horizontal drain pipe running through the dike that makes the spillway. When the water level rises above the 2-inch, open-topped stand-pipe, the water drains down and through to the overflow side of the spillway.

If you want to keep ducks or geese, an island provides some protection from predators, and in a large pond the bulldozer can use the soil from the hole to make the island.

A good-sized bulldozer with operator usually costs from $60 to $80 an hour. An experienced contractor can give you a good estimate as to how many hours it will take to do the job you have staked out. If he should hit a ledge of rock or other obstacle, it will take more time.

Let's say the pool is dug and nicely filled in the spring, but as summer comes on it begins to go dry faster than would be expected from evaporation alone. This probably means that there is a leak in the bottom that should be fixed. You could, however, choose to let the pond "sit" for another season before taking dramatic (and expensive) action to stop the leak. It may seal itself. The silt that washes in from the surrounding land sifts down to the bottom and may fill the spaces between the minute shingle-like plates of which clay is composed.

What to Do if It Leaks

If the leak persists, there are three ways to approach the problem: you can compact the bottom, add a sealant or line the pond with plastic. First pump out or otherwise drain the pond and look for gravelly places that might be letting water through. Add a little water to the pond and perhaps you can see where it is leaking out. In fact, when the pond is first dug, you should look carefully for places where the clay covering seems thin or non-existent. Make a sketch or photograph so you will know where to check first if a leak should develop.

The easiest method of repair is to compact the clay bottom. This calls for a contractor with a sheeps-foot roller. This is a heavy piece of equipment with flat foot-like protuberances on the roller for maximum compression of the soil. You have probably seen them used for compacting fill in highway construction. If possible, add a layer of clay to the bottom before compacting the area.

For more difficult situations, where there is simply not enough clay content for successful compaction, the addition of a material called Bentonite may be required. This is a dry powder that expands up to seven times its bulk when wet and in the process can seal the minute spaces in the clay through which the water may be leaking.

Spread the Bentonite on a reasonably dry bottom at the rate of about two to three pounds per square yard and rake it in thoroughly before filling the pond. The material is available through building-supply and garden stores.

As a final measure a pool can be lined with sheet plastic. Polyethelene about 8 mil in thickness is recommended for a big pool. The seams can be taped or chemically welded.

When the pool is shaped to your liking, all sticks and stones should be raked out and the surface made smooth. Then spread 2 or 3 inches of sand over the sides and bottom as a cushion for the plastic liner. This may seem to be a lot of trouble but irregularities in the bottom can chafe a hole through the liner—and one small leak is more than enough.

If you know that the soil below the liner contains peat, humus or other decomposing matter, do not use a liner. The gas that forms from decomposition can raise the liner off the bottom.

If the top edges of the plastic are tucked well into the soil just below the average water level, the plastic will not be obvious to the eye. When the pond is finished and filled, the raw earth around the edges should be raked and shaped to a pleasing profile and planted to suit your taste. Willow trees *(Salix babylonica)* are natural companions to a pond. Red dogwood *(Cornus stolonifera)* and huckleberry *(Vaccinium corymbosum)* look good together and do well in moist places—particularly in the cooler climates. Day-lilies *(Hemerocallis)* are colorful, remarkably easy to care for and also do well beside a stream. For detailed lists of plants to use, see Part II, Chapters 1 and 2.

The plantings should look reasonably natural, which means using larger drifts of fewer plants instead of a wide variety of species planted in spots. Make the plantings big and bold enough to relate well to the site. The pond will be visible from a considerable distance. The plantings that are used should also be visible from a distance. Here, again, a matter of scale is to be considered. Consider it well.

Grass, which grows quickly and is relatively inexpensive, is the obvious ground cover to use around a pond. If you are not sure what will do well in the soil and conditions of climate and moisture on the perimeter of the pond, try a mixture of a number of kinds. One owner of a country place about 60 miles north of New York City simply scattered a seed mixture of trefoil, alfalfa, rye, timothy and orchard grass and harrowed it in. Two years later the area was covered and all the grasses were still in evidence, some doing better than others where the conditions were more suitable for their needs.

Ponds, like gardens, start to change as soon as they are created, which is part of their fascination. The natural impetus of a garden is to return to a state of wilderness. And that is what it will become unless controlled by the hand of man. The natural impetus of a pond is to fill up and become land. And that is what it will become in time—unless it is cleaned (weeded) and controlled.

The natural process of filling up is inevitable and watching it is one of the pleasures of having a pond. If it is fed by the runoff of ground water, microscopic (and often much larger) pieces of soil are introduced into the water. These pieces in the form of silt are deposited in certain areas depending on the water current. As the silt builds up the water becomes more shallow, and moisture-loving grasses will find a seed bed and start to grow. The grasses will thrive for their season and die down, making the area more shallow and more suitable for other plants that do well in shallow situations.

Cattails, ferns, maples, milkweed and skunk cabbage will take hold, and the area slowly becomes more like a bog than a pond. This is a process that takes years, and it can be stopped by digging out the pond at any time. It is interesting, however, to let the progression develop in one small area at least.

Frogs, turtles, snails, water snakes and kingfishers are among the animals that like water and are likely to appear.

The pleasures of a pond are many and varied. Where you see cattails standing stark against the background of hill or water, you will surely see redwing blackbirds perching on them. The frogs will set up a nightly chorus. A flight of ducks or geese will come sailing in some evening. Lay a log along the edge and the turtles will climb aboard to bask in the sun. You can stock the pond with fish to catch for the pan. Pleasant thoughts like these are especially helpful when you get the bill for the back-hoe and bulldozer.

The spacing of the water lilies and the varied plants and grasses on the shore help to give this man-made pool a lovely natural look.

5

The Natural Look and the Man-Made

If you are blessed with a natural pond, you are fortunate indeed and need only be encouraged to treasure it and show it off to best advantage in the landscape. Consider the possibility of opening up lines of sight from the house and outdoor living areas, so that the water can be seen. Use plantings in natural-looking clusters on the far edge of the pond from the usual viewing angle. This helps establish an edge and holds the eye to the focal point—which is the water of the pond itself. Consider putting in more fish, frogs and turtles for they can add another dimension to the enjoyment of the pond. For more on this, refer to Part III, Chapter 2.

You may also want to check the chapter on water lilies to see whether or not they could be grown in your pond.

If the pond is stream-fed, you will probably have to do some digging-out of silt and sand, especially after heavy rainfall.

In some cases, by the diversion of more water from the downspouts on one side of the house, or by occasional filling with a hose, a boggy low spot can be made into a small pond. If the pond is filled with surface water, a sheet of polyethelene will help hold it. If the pond is filled with ground water, the plastic liner will tend to keep it out.

You can make the water look as natural as possible, or you can establish a hard edge of brick, flagstones or concrete and make it obviously more decorative and formal—and obviously man-made.

The Natural Look

If a natural pond is what you prefer, the best possible model is nature herself. If you don't know of any ponds in your area, check with a good road map and see if there are some within driving distance in parks or forest preserves. When you go to see them concentrate especially on what happens around the edges. Is there an area of sandy beach or gravel? Is there a ledge of rock or are individual rocks grouped along the edge? Does grass or sedge grow into the shallow water? How do the plants seem to space themselves around the pond? Is the bottom of mud, clay or sand? How steeply does it slope away from the bank?

What about the outline, is it symmetrical or asymmetrical? Is the edge a straight arc or rather scalloped in effect? Factors such as these, and everything else you can see and, preferably, write down, about a few natural ponds will give you a basis for deciding what you like best. You can then incorporate the most appealing aspects of the natural look to the pond you plan in your own back yard.

Plants for the Edges

Finding the plants may not be easy, and it is illegal almost everywhere to gather plants from the wild. But if you know the general appearance of the plants that looked good to you in the wild (or have pictures of them), you will have a good idea of what to seek out when shopping in a nursery. The nurseryman will tell you which of the plants he sells will take wet and boggy conditions.

Keep in mind, too, that if you like the looks of a plant and would like to grow it beside a pond or stream, even if not suited to wet soil, it can be planted on a gently sloping mound built alongside. This has to be large enough to accommodate the mature root system of the plant, which means it cannot be an insignificant incident on the land-scape. The mound must be large enough to provide a literal as well as a visual base for the planting. In the section on plants, below, you will find descriptions of many kinds from which you can choose.

Relate the Pool to the Surroundings

Let's say that you have decided to have a small pond or pool with a few plants around the edge and perhaps some water lilies growing in it. And let's say you have decided exactly where you want it to be and what size. (Some thoughts on the matter of size are given later.) The next question is, what character do you want the pool to have? Should it look somewhat as if it occurred naturally on the landscape or should it look definitely and obviously man-made? You will find the answer in the surroundings. If you live on a city street, perhaps in a tract of houses with lots of pavement and few trees, a naturalistic pool will seem out of place. In such a situation, stay in character with the paving and hard edges all around and make a pool more formal than natural or informal. "Formal" in this sense simply means obviously planned and fitted rather symmetrically into the total scheme of things. Formal design is traditionally balanced equally on each side of a central line or axis.

An informal pool, on the other hand, will look most at home where the property lines are not too obviously rectangular, where there are relatively few hard and rigid edges of paving, and where there are enough trees and shrubs so that a small pool with a woodland appearance will not seem hopelessly lost or out of place.

Of course, even in the most gridlike of subdivisions, there may be a corner of a lot planted with a woodland look where a natural pool would not be incongruous. It is all a matter of personal taste. If the pool seems appropriate to its immediate surroundings, you will probably be happier with it than if it looks obviously inappropriate.

The pool should be large enough to be the obvious major feature in its immediate setting but not so large as to be overwhelming. The "setting" is the immediately surrounding area that will visually "belong" to the pool when you look at it.

It is within this established space that the pool, or terrace, or raised bed, or walk or any other landscape feature must fit comfortably.

To simulate the size of a pool you can put down sheets of clear plastic to indicate the water and pieces of 2 by 4 to indicate the coping. If the pool is to be informal, without coping, a length of rope or hose can simulate the edge.

Make the plastic the shape and size you think you want and hold it down, if necessary, with giant U-shaped staples made from metal coat hangers. Then live with the layout for a few days. Look at it from every possible angle of view and get a feel for the way it relates to the site. Your neighbors may wonder about the plastic patch on the lawn, but there is no better way to visualize exactly how the size of the pool will fit in the area allotted.

The Mound Cascade and Waterfall

So far we have been concerned mostly with water on the level, except for a falls that might be established in the run of a stream. A more dramatic display can be created on a slope or mound with a small cascade.

If you have a high spot in an appropriate place in the garden, it can be increased by bringing in fill dirt to make a mound that will serve as a foundation for a small display of water.

Even if your plot of land is as flat as a billiard table, you can create a mound or two or three and use one of them for a display of water. This creation of slopes and mounds for added sculptural interest is a valid landscape concept whether or not a water feature is added.

This is not an easy job if you do it yourself, and is not inexpensive if you have it done by professionals. But, if done well, it can add an entirely new perspective to your view of the garden.

The best time to sculpt the land for added interest is when the site is being graded or at least

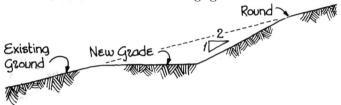

In making an excavation to provide a level area, do not overlook the question of where to put the soil that must be taken away. If possible use it for filling elsewhere.

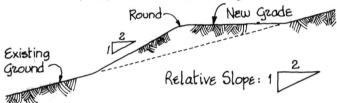

In building an embankment to establish a level area, the slope should not exceed a relationship of one foot in rise to each two feet of length. If the relative slope exceeds this ratio, the soil may slip and the level not hold.

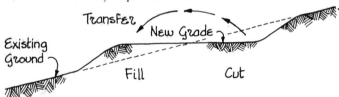

Where possible, plan the leveling of a slope so that the amount of cut will be in balance with the amount of fill.

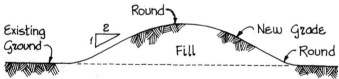

The critical factor in making a mound is to establish a slope on all sides that does not exceed the natural angle of repose of the soil. Rounding, as indicated here, will also help to stabilize the mound.

before the lawn is put in. If you can decide what you want and where you want it at that time, a cooperative bull-dozer operator can build small back yard mountains to fit your needs.

If the slopes are to be covered with grass, they should be gentle enough to prevent fast runoff when the lawn is watered. If you plan to build a cascade faced with rock, the slope can be as steep as you would like it. The mounds you see in the picture above are about 6 feet across and 2-1/2 feet high, enough to make a significant impact in an intimate space just a few feet from a terrace, as these are. But to make a meaningful mark on the land at the back of a large lot, say for viewing at a distance of 50 or 60 feet, the mound should be 3 to 4 feet high and three to four times as wide. To make a mound 3 feet high and 9 feet across takes about 5 cubic yards of dirt. This comes to some 70 trips with a garden wheelbarrow carrying 2 cubic feet (about 200 pounds). Keep this consideration in mind before you start such a project.

When the mound is roughly established, the waterway can be installed. In climates where freezing and thawing are not a problem, the rocks over which the water will run can be set firmly in place and soil tamped down around them to hold them in place. At least two-thirds of the bulk of the rock should be set into the slope, with no more than one-third projecting.

In cold climates the rock must be set solidly in a core of concrete. This is expensive, however, and unless all aspects of drainage are carefully considered, the stone can still break loose from the concrete in a hard freeze. Unless you are practiced in working with concrete, it is probably best to use the "dry wall" technique. This is the way stone walls are made in New England, and they have stood true under rigorous winter temperatures for a hundred years. The stones are laid without mortar, so water cannot collect between them and freeze and expand and move the wall. They are, in effect, self-draining.

A cascade can be essentially a sloping stone wall built by this method, with relatively little soil involved.

Rock Work

The rocks should be laid so the water will take the most showy course from the source at the top to the catch basin at the bottom. The basin can be a ready-made pool of plastic, a pool lined with sheet plastic or one made with concrete.

The only sure way to check the flow of water as the stone is laid from the bottom up is to test it rock by rock with water from the hose as the rock is laid up.

To accommodate the recirculation pump, the pool should be about a foot deep. The plastic tubing that carries the water from the catch basin back to the top of the fall should be installed as the rock spillway is put in. With care, it can be put in so it will not show.

The size of the pump required will depend on how high you want the cascade to be and what volume of water you would like to see cascading down. In Part I, Chapter 7 on recirculating pumps there is information as to what pump and tubing sizes are required to lift different volumes of water to different heights.

The flow of the cascade should be in a pleasing proportion to the amount of rock in the spillway. The most common mistake is to create too much masonry and have too little water cascading down. The water, not the masonry, should dominate the setting.

The Full-Scale Waterfall

The creation of a display that approximates the size and character of a natural waterfall is a major undertaking, but it can be a delightful addition to a garden.

To get a satisfying effect, there must be a considerable fall. Anything less than 4 feet would be questionable for a truly natural effect. And if the area (and the budget) are large enough, a fall of 6 to 8 feet is more to the scale that makes a definite and impressive statement on the subject of falling water.

Unless you are fortunate enough to have a steep outcropping of rock or a slope that can be cut back and faced with stone to make a clear drop of a satisfactory height, do not strive for a "natural" waterfall. Unless the conditions are such that the illusion can be reasonably well realized, it is better to face the fact that the fall is artificial and proceed to make it as attractive as possible without regard to the natural look. The sound and the splash and the endless variety of shifting patterns in the fall of the water are the pleasures to be attained, and these you will get if the water falls for the required distance in sufficient volume.

A large fall usually looks best in front of a sizable background of large evergreen shrubs or small trees. On most suburban sites this would put it at the back edge of the lot or in a corner. Even

This man-made fall in the Climatron in St. Louis shows the degree of reality that can be attained with a pump and good design.

an obviously man-made fall can profit from some implied relationship to nature. The masonry structure over which the water flows cannot rise like a stone cairn or pylon of brick and seem at home in a suburban garden. And, even if obviously artificial, there should be a pleasing relation to the landscape and the sense of water coming from a secret or distant place and flowing over an edge into a pool below.

The character of the fall of water is controlled by the edge over which it spills. The top of the falls, literally the spillway, can be wide so the water drops in a thin sheet that will vary with the wind and through which you can see the material behind the fall. As the width of the spillway is narrowed (assuming the same volume of water), the fall increases in density and becomes a more solid column of water.

Keep in mind the character you want the falling water to have and design the spillway and the receptacle below so as to achieve this essential quality. But you won't really know how it is going to work until the pump is started and the water begins to flow. Then is the time for the necessary fine-tuning with rock and mortar to make the fall just the way you want it.

Adding Water to a Wall

The classic way to use the vertical surface of a wall for a display of water is the wall fountain. It is a method that is still hard to beat.

If there is a high wall of stone, brick or concrete block, a fall of water can often be gracefully added. A projection can be made and water piped to flow over the edge. The effectiveness and desirability of such an addition can easily be determined by experimenting with the water from a garden hose. The hose may not deliver the preferred volume that a good-sized circulation pump could provide, but it will show the effect.

Some of the basic concepts for designing with water in other situations also apply here. Nature is obviously the best place to observe the ways of water falling and the character of the environment in which it occurs. Pictures of natural falls will be of help in establishing a natural character for whatever you may do at home. Even two or three rocks can be placed together in ways that are natural and comfortable to see. They can also be awkwardly placed. The clues to the natural way are to be found in nature.

Make the framework for the fall as attractive and interesting as possible without the water. The size and shape should be in scale with the setting, and the forms, colors and textures should be well organized and related. The dry fountain, in short, should be considered as a piece of sculpture, and the water will simply give it an added dimension.

In making a waterfall, the shapes and sizes of the stones must be carefully chosen and firmly set so they will overlap and interlock to hold them securely in place.

The Drama of Water in Vertical Form

In nature the vertical display of water is the province of Old Faithful and Moby Dick. In the garden a water jet is obviously the work of man in defiance of the law of gravity. We tend to dramatize our few small victories over natural forces, and there is no doubt about the drama of water standing in a column to the height of its head of pressure and falling back upon itself in ever-changing bursts and bubbles.

Fortunately, the free-standing jet of water is an easy effect to attain. All that's required is a catch basin in which a recirculating pump and appropriate fountain fixture can be set, and an electrical outlet into which the pump can be safely plugged. The mechanics of installation are explained below. The first consideration is where and how to relate the fountain to the setting.

A small jet-fountain can go almost anywhere. It can be used as a supportive accent beside an entryway, at the edge of a terrace, at the end of a low garden wall or beside the landing of a flight of garden steps. As with any other small accent, a piece of sculpture, a dramatic rock or piece of driftwood is more effective visually if tied to some structural element in the garden design. A little time spent visualizing such a feature in various parts of your own garden will illustrate the point that, if not tied to some established element, it may seem lost and isolated.

Some Thoughts About Relative Scale

A larger fountain, however, can stand alone and become a focal point in itself, to which other elements can be tied. The fountain can be situated on an axis—lined up with the edge or center of a terrace—at the back of the lot lined up with the back door. It might also be set in one corner of a back yard with, perhaps, a semicircle of evergreens behind it as a backdrop. As with all other elements in the garden, the fountain must be in pleasing scale with all that is around it.

This matter of scale is subtle and all-important. Good designers, through years of practice, can tell what size various parts of a design should be for proper relationships. In simplest terms, and not so ridiculous as it sounds, a thing is in good scale when it doesn't look too large, or too small, in its setting. This is not so hard to determine after a thing is in place; the trick is to get the size right before it is built, planted or installed.

In planning a fountain one can readily make a mockup to see how it will look in the chosen location. If this model is about the size you intend to have, it will give you an idea of the scale as well.

A garden hose can be used to make a circle the size of the intended basin. An upright piece of 2 by 2 lumber can represent the height of the water jet. If a square splash basin is planned, use 2 by 2's or, for smaller installations, pieces of lath to lay out the size of the base.

When the mockup is in place, leave it for a few days so you can see it from every angle. As you would for any other garden feature, such as a planting bed or flowering tree, consider the view through major windows in the house, for perhaps it can be placed so that it can be enjoyed from inside as well as out.

Look at the fountain in relation to the sunlight at different times of day. Water is particularly beautiful when backlighted by the sun. The droplets become prisms that glisten and reflect. You can prove this by tying a garden hose to an upright stake and walking around it when the sun is low on the horizon. You will see how dramatically the effect of the water is changed by front light, side light and back light.

This may well seem like a lot of trouble for a little jet of water, but you will never get the most out of it if you don't know what "the most" is.

We have been concerned here with a simple jet of water rising from a pool or splash basin. The

Pool
Too large

About right

Too small

Good scale is essentially a matter of creating a pleasant balance in the size of related objects.

effect depends largely on the flow of water. This is the simplest kind of fountain. Endless possibilities include more ambitious classic formal fountains that may be quite attractive as sculptural forms, with water used as an added dimension.

This is what probably comes to mind when one first thinks of a fountain. In its basic form it usually has a round pool at the base with a raised edge. In the center is a column rising through the middle of two or three shallow saucers of diminishing size. The saucers are often scalloped at the edges. Water bubbles or sprays up through the top and splashes down all around from the saucers into the base. This is the classic fountain for public places and large estates. It ranges in size from moderate to monumental. It loses its effect, however, when too small. These fountains are well suited only to a formal (symmetrical) landscape arrangement and are at their best where the size and character of the house as well as the garden are such that an imposing fountain would not look out of place.

The free-standing jet of water is the most dramatic and one of the easiest effects to achieve.

6

Small Pools
That Are Easy to Make

Few indeed are the do-it-yourself projects that
offer so much satisfaction for such a modest
investment of time and expense as the making of
a small decorative pool. As you will see on the following pages, they can be made of a variety of
materials. There are ideas included here for making pools of concrete, brick, wood, concrete block
and, easiest of all, the ready-made plastic liners
available in many garden supply stores.

The material need not match the surroundings,
but there should be a pleasing relationship. If you
have a brick terrace, the pool could well be made
of concrete, wood or brick. Concrete block does
not relate well to brick, but it's a good choice if
the patio is concrete or the house is stucco or concrete block. There are no hard-and-fast rules
about mixing materials, but it pays to try to visualize the results before you decide on the material to use.

Again, in the construction of a pool, the matter
of getting it the right size for its setting (relative
scale) must be carefully considered. There is a
thorough discussion of this important aspect of
design in Part I, Chapter 5.

If you plan to grow aquatic plants, and they are
one of the good reasons for building a pool, you
should review the chapter on choosing and planting. You can then design the pool to accommodate
properly the plants you want to grow.

Specific dimensions are not given on the sketches that follow because these pools can be made to fit the space you have for them in the garden. Most of them are within the scope of anyone reasonably handy with tools. But if they seem too complicated, part or all of the work could be let out to a professional. All wiring, of course, should be done by a qualified electrician.

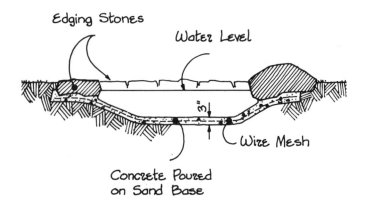

Edging Stones

Water Level

Wire Mesh

Concrete Poured
on Sand Base

For a Natural Setting

If you live in a very cold climate, check with the concrete supplier to see whether the three-inch reinforced concrete bottom will be enough to withstand the local conditions of freezing and thawing. For a pool larger than three feet across, there should be a drain for emptying. Note that the rock coping is set into the concrete.

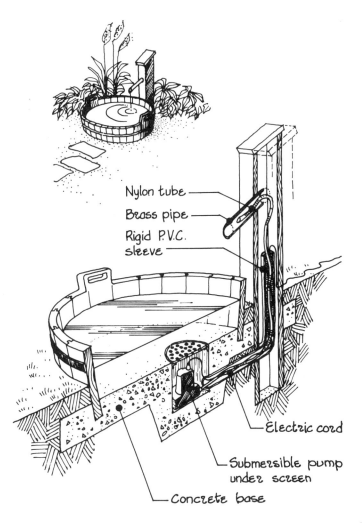

Nylon tube

Brass pipe

Rigid P.V.C.
sleeve

Electric cord

Submersible pump
under screen

Concrete base

This is an attractive pool for a country place. The flow of water need not be large and a small pump will do a good job. Where the wood touches the soil it should be treated with preservative, and it will last for many years. If it does rot out, which it will eventually do in wet climates, it can be replaced. If you can find an old tub or half barrel to use, so much the better. If not, a circular container can be made. It will be much easier to do, however, if the sides are made straight instead of sloping. Notice the screen in the bottom over the pump. This is important to keep the inlet from plugging up.

**The Old-Time
Look**

This is typical concrete construction for a small raised pool that would probably look best in a contemporary garden. The sketch at upper left shows a flow of water which would be activated by an in-line pump screened by the rocks and planting. The cross section shows how the wood forms would be set in place before the concrete is poured.

Clean Lines in Concrete

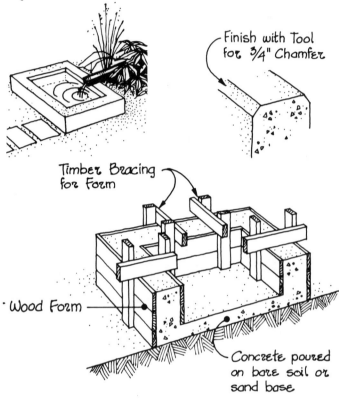

Finish with Tool
for 3/4" Chamfer

Timber Bracing
for Form

Wood Form

Concrete poured
on bare soil or
sand base

This bowl, which can be used in a number of ways, is simply poured over a mound of earth, as shown in the cross-section drawing. Make the circular mound the size you want, plaster on some concrete, put in wire mesh and add more on the outside (actually the bottom of the basin) as required for the thickness you want. Note the angle of the edge where it is formed against the base of the mound. The bowl will have an interesting rough texture reflecting that of the soil on which it is formed. To create a similar texture on the outside, soil can be sprinkled on before concrete sets.

Simple Basin of Concrete

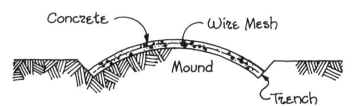

Concrete poured over mound – Cross Section

Basin turned right side up

Metal pools for an arrangement such as this are available commercially. So are plastic pools, but they seldom look at home in a garden. Again, a recirculation pump is at work.

For Subtle Sounds

Poured
Concrete

The cross sections show the elements of construction for pools using a variety of different materials. The marginal sketches show what a corner detail would look like when the job is finished. The concrete would require a form, of course, and it can be framed as shown on page 50. The sand base will help prevent freezing and thawing under the pool but in climates where the winters are hard, reinforcement should be used in accordance with local custom.

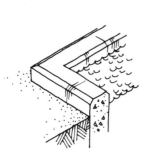
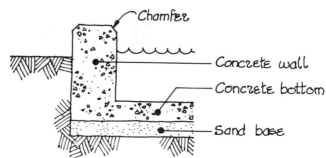

Brick
Masonry

Brick is even more susceptible to frost-heaving than concrete and the best way to prevent leaking, in climates where freezing is a problem, is to install a plastic membrane between the brick bottom of the pool and the sand base upon which the brick is set. Note that the membrane goes around the sides as well. The bricks are simply stacked in place and no mortar is used to hold them.

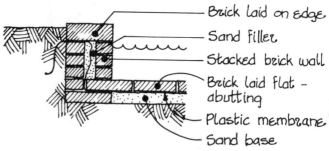

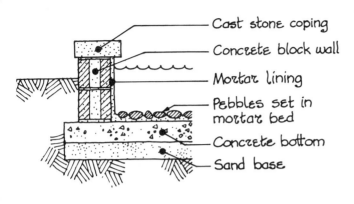

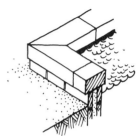

Concrete Block

Concrete block is another material that is at home only in a modern garden setting. It does not seem right for the garden of a traditional house. Block is not hard to work with, the pieces are larger than brick and fewer are required. In this project, however, there is considerable masonry work to be done and one should have some experience before taking it on. Unless the masonry yard can provide a 45-degree corner as shown, it would be best to butt two pieces together.

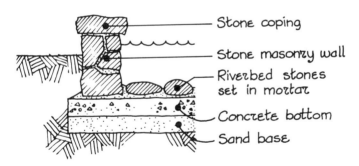

Stone Masonry

A pool lined and edged with stone is ideal for a traditional garden setting. It is not easy to find the stone, unless you live where old stone walls are being taken down for housing developments. The selection of the stone and the setting in place is a time-consuming job, but a rewarding one if you have the patience for it. Note that the capstones overhang the wall, and that the bottom is lined with rock.

Using Railroad Ties

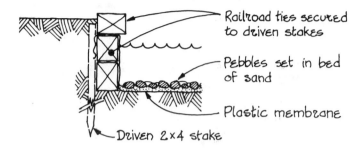

Railroad ties secured to driven stakes

Pebbles set in bed of sand

Plastic membrane

Driven 2×4 stake

Railroad ties, where available, are of a size and shape that makes it quick and easy to create a fair-sized pool, as shown here. The plastic membrane is used to hold the water in place. The membrane goes under the sand on the bottom and the pebbles on the sand provide an interesting texture. The top tie is turned the wide way to make an overhang and shadow line.

Plastic Liner with Stone Edge

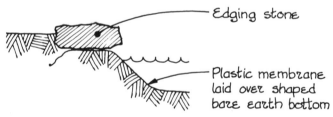

Edging stone

Plastic membrane laid over shaped bare earth bottom

The easiest of all to make, and a very attractive one, is this pool made with a plastic membrane. It comes in kit form from various suppliers, and is lined with rocks set around the edge. The earth should be cleaned of all sticks and rocks and if it is rough a layer of sand could be put under the plastic to keep it from being cut or torn. A thin layer of sand under the rock edge will provide further protection.

The alga is a plant that grows in an amazing range of sizes and shapes. The brown kelp of the Pacific and other large seaweeds are algae as is the green scum that will probably develop in a sunny spot in your pond or pool. In the latter form it is far from attractive and should be eliminated.

The minute airborne spores of algae will develop into the green scum wherever there is enough sunlight on the surface and sufficient nutrients (mineral salts) in the water.

What You Should Know About Algae

An obvious algae control is to have your pool in the shade but this is not conducive to the growing of lilies. You can, however, make sure that nutrients such as plant food, leaf mold, compost or fish food are not used in excess. As these materials decompose they release the mineral salts that encourage the growth of algae.

The underwater oxygenating plants will utilize some of the nutrients and will also absorb some of the sunlight and thus inhibit the development of algae. You will find a list of these worthwhile plants on page 104. Tadpoles and snails will feed on algae so they, too, should be encouraged if you have the problem.

Various chemicals will kill algae but the best is copper sulphate (blue vitriol). This is a dangerous poison and must be used with extreme care. Some pool suppliers offer it under various trade names. Just be sure to follow the instructions to the letter. The usual recommendation is to put the crystals in a cotton bag, such as a Bull Durham tobacco bag. Tie it to a pole with a string and swish it through the water. There's danger of damage to fish and plants if more than minute quantities are used. In a pool 10 feet by 10 feet, 3 feet deep (which contains about 1100 gallons of water), no more that 1/5 of a *dram* should be used, and a dram is only 1/16th of an ounce. Use the chemical very sparingly and if the algae persists after a week or so, use it sparingly again at weekly intervals until it is gone.

Look to Nature for Design

*These rocks were piled
up to slow the water and
make a wading pool.
The dam is obviously
made by man.*

*A similar pool, done in
nature's way. There are
no straight lines and each
rock sits firmly in place.
These are two principles
to observe when working
with rocks in water.*

7

What You Should Know About Recirculating Pumps

Water in motion can be a truly fascinating garden attraction. Where nature has failed to oblige with a ready brook or waterfall, man can step in with plumbing and a recirculating pump to create any number of moving water effects—cascades, springs, spouts or fountains. In a recirculating system the same amount of water is used over and over again. No new water has to be added except to make up for depletion caused by natural evaporation.

A recirculation pump is used to transport water from a low pool to a high point from where the water returns by gravity to the low pool in a continuing cycle. In the low pool the water is drawn into the pump through a screened intake. At the high point it is discharged from the discharge pipe. At the point of discharge the water can be passed through a nozzle or system of nozzles to create a jet or other spray pattern. The path of return to the low pool can be manipulated to create a number of interesting effects—a waterfall, a series of cascades, a gutter with a flume or a simulated brook. The falling water can be made to turn a waterwheel.

A number of ready-to-use, easy-to-install recirculating pumps are on the market at moderate prices. They are available both in submersible or open-air (also called in-line) models. The submersibles are fully sealed for direct permanent underwater operation. Many submersible models are also suitable for in-line operation.

Types of Pumps

Submerged Pump

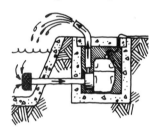

In-Line Pump

All elements of a submersible pump are efficiently sealed so it will operate safely under water. Pumps that are not designed to run under water must be installed in a separate box or pit and connected to the line of flow.

The more popular models are electric motor pumps that plug into any grounded 110/120-volt outlet on a general purpose domestic circuit. The submersible pumps are the simplest to operate and require no more installation effort than to set them (no fastening or bolts required) on the bottom of the pool, attach the recirculation tube and to plug them in. In-line pumps use an additional intake tube and have to be placed outside the pool but usually lower than the water surface. A point to keep in mind, however: any extension of electric circuits or installation of new outlets should be made by a qualified electrician.

The best feature of a submersible recirculation system is that it is a self-contained package that can be installed or removed independently of any other plumbing or construction. It fits into any type of pool or basin. There are no design requirements other than that the water containing the pump be deep enough to be about 3 to 4 inches above the top of the pump. The smaller pump units only weigh from about 3 to 5 pounds and are about 6 to 8 inches high by 7 to 10 inches across.

In selecting a pump for your water feature, you should first determine the type—whether submerged or in-line—that would be preferable on the basis of its most practical location and the intended plumbing arrangement. A submerged pump would afford a simpler plumbing system, but in order to conceal it in shallow water, it would have to be placed in a screened or covered sump. Where this is impractical, perhaps because of bedrock or other obstructions, you may decide on an in-line unit.

Pump Capacity

Your next basis of selection should be pump capacity—flow and lift. Flow is the amount of fluid a pump can deliver in a given unit of time against a given head (head is the vertical distance between pump intake and discharge) and for small recirculating pumps is commonly expressed in gallons

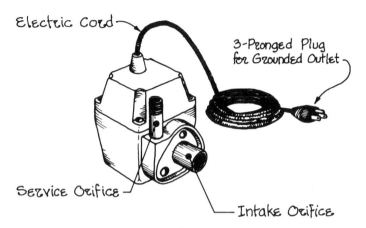

The submersible pumps available today are remarkably compact. Only the inlet and outlet (service orifice) are open.

per hour. Lift is the head against which the pump is capable of delivering a given flow. The two are inversely proportional. A pump capable of delivering 90 gallons per hour against a head of 3 feet might deliver only, say, 60 gallons per hour against a 5-foot head.

When ordering a pump, you should make sure it will be a size capable of doing the work required. You will find the necessary information on the manufacturer's stated flow-lift ratio. This is commonly specified in gallons per hour delivered at varying heads. For sprays or fountains you should also obtain the pump's spray height capability for the desired nozzle opening or fountain head. Next you should make sure the electrical outlet will meet the pump's voltage and amperage requirements. It is advisable to choose a model bearing the Underwriter's Laboratory approved label.

Your flow and lift requirements can easily be determined in advance. For lift requirements, simply measure the vertical distance from the point at which the pump would be drawing water and the intended point of discharge. For flow determination, for example, of a water cascade—after completing the cascade construction—provide water from a garden hose at a flow rate that looks right. Then intercept the entire flow at some point between the upper and lower pools by placing, say, an open one-gallon container under one of the waterfalls. If it takes 15 seconds to fill the container, then your flow requirements will be 3,600 divided by 15 (the filling time in seconds) or 240 gallons per hour.

A jet or a fountain, too, can be simulated with a garden hose. By catching the jet in a container either before it hits the pool or by letting the pool overflow into the container and measuring the time it takes to fill the container, the rate of flow can be computed as for the cascade. If the container is larger or smaller than one gallon, go through the same procedure but multiply the gallons per hour by the number of (or fraction of) gallons in the container.

Maintenance

Maintenance requirements for a recirculating pump, too, should be checked out before the time of purchase. Many small recirculating pumps are guaranteed for a certain time of operation with practically no maintenance other than occasional back flushing with clean water. Most, however, are not suited to be left submerged or in an active line during severe winter weather.

Plumbing

In addition to the pump, all the plumbing required for a simple recirculating arrangement is a length of plastic tube from the pump's service orifice to the intended point of discharge and whatever clamps may be required to attach the tube and secure it on its way. Submersible recir-

culating pumps normally come complete with a
screened intake and, for best results, should be
placed into a sump or at the lowest point in the
pool. For in-line operation, another tube with a
screen on the end must be provided for the
pump's intake orifice.

That's all there is to it. Simply set the pump
(provided it is a submersible unit) in the pool bottom. Attach the discharge tube to the service
opening of the pump. Run the tube along its
intended path and secure the discharge end in the
desired position and in a way that the water will
ultimately flow back into the pool. Make sure the
pool is filled with water, take the pump's electric
cord to the nearest grounded outlet and plug it
in. Flow and force of flow at the discharge point
can then be regulated by placing an adjustable
constricting clamp over the flexible plastic discharge tube and leaving it at the desired setting.

Installation

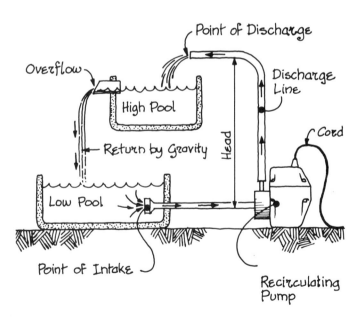

*This sketch shows how water is recirculated to provide a
constant fall. The "head" is the height it is raised.*

The length of the overflow pipe determines the depth of the water. It also provides easy drainage without the need for a valve.

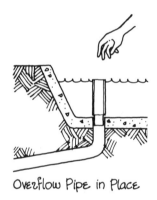

Overflow Pipe in Place

Overflow Pipe Removed

The recirculation tubing and the pump's electric cord can either be left to lie on the pool bottom and on the ground or they can be concealed under earth, rocks, planting or in statuary.

Nozzles for fountain heads are available in both metal and plastic in a great variety of spray patterns. They should be attached to the free end of the discharge tube and can be mounted on standpipes, on rocks, or built into statuary in an infinite number of ways. Complete ready-for-installation pool-and-fountain kits, too, are on the market for the less ambitious do-it-yourselfer.

Normally no plumbing is required to fill or to drain a small garden pool. The pool can be filled simply with a garden hose and drained by a garden hose siphon or, if it is a separate basin, by tipping. The submersible pump can also be used to empty the pool. Simply catch the flow in a bucket and empty where convenient. As a matter of convenience, however, many garden pool owners prefer to install more sophisticated plumbing to fill and drain the pool or to regulate its water level.

An overflow system is advisable to prevent uncontrolled flooding as may be caused by heavy rains. The overflow can be provided either in the form of a weir (spillway) or it can be combined with a pool drain. To save time and for ease of cleaning, garden pools and larger basins should be provided with a permanent drain leading from the lowest point in the pool bottom to either a dry well, catch basin or surface drainage course. The drain can be simply plugged with a plug-and-chain as in a bathtub or it can be provided with a slip-in overflow pipe. This overflow pipe is inserted into the drain vertically and should be of a length so that, when in place, its upper end will be at the intended normal water level. While effectively plugging the drain inlet itself, it permits any excess water to drain out through its open end at the top. To drain the pool, the over-flow pipe is simply pulled out of the drain-pipe.

A more elaborate drain-overflow system consists of a main drain with a valve and a side overflow drain that connects to the main drain below the valve which, of course, is normally closed. The valve should be placed in the drain line outside the pool perimeter. The valve is opened only to drain the pool.

A permanent water line can be installed to fill the pool simply by turning a valve handle. In dry climates where evaporation tends to continually lower the pool level, an automatic level control system can be provided. The valve in the inlet line, instead of being manually operated, would be

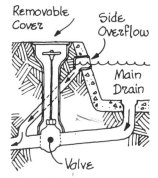

If you do not want a visible pipe, the overflow can be installed in the side of the pool and the drain controlled by a valve (or by a plug in the bottom).

The pleasing effect of waterside plantings in a pool such as this depends upon maintaining a constant water level. This calls for a sufficient volume of flow and an overflow at the right height. A side drain is best for a naturalized pool.

activated by a float on a lever or "arm." This system works on the same principle as the device that keeps your water closet tank filled and ready for flushing. When the water drops to a predetermined level, the float arm opens the valve. As the float rises with the water level, it returns to the position that causes the valve to be shut again.

Before installing a recirculation system, you should be able to answer the following questions:

1. Is the lower pool large enough and deep enough for a submerged pump?
2. If not, where would you place an in-line pump?
3. Where is your nearest grounded electric outlet? What voltage, amperage available?
4. What are your lift and flow requirements?

This small cascade creates a most satisfying sound and it is operated by means of an in-line pump.

8

Using Lights with Water, Plants and Stone

Light can be a landscape element as critical to the success of a garden as are its earth forms, its water, plants and rocks. Dark and bright areas interact to form a lightscape just as the interaction of mass and space forms the basic landscape. Gardening with light, therefore, requires every bit as much thought and effort as does the basic landscape design. The designer of the lightscape, however, has an advantage in that most garden lighting systems can be designed by trial and error. Before they are permanently installed, garden lights can be moved around until the effect is right.

Different landscape elements, water, plants or rocks react in different ways to different types of lights. Since most gardens are composed of combinations of several of these elements, good lighting design requires experience. A light fixture placed to highlight, say, a garden pool could easily have the wrong effect on the appearance of adjacent rocks or plants.

The skillful use of lights extends a garden's beauty into the night and adds unsuspected new dimensions to its features. The garden can be turned into a chiaroscuro nightscape of deep shadows, soft glows, starlike sparkles, sculptural silhouettes and occasional highlights. The importance of the dark elements—shadows and silhouettes—is too often overlooked in an effort to light a garden. Too much light tends to reduce and confuse depth perception and renders the eye insensitive to the nocturnal ambience. Thus by overlighting, the subtlety of the garden setting can easily be lost. Restraint is the key to getting a good start on a garden lighting scheme.

Types of Lights

A variety of light sources can be used. The simplest, perhaps, are candles in hurricane chimneys on stands or in lanterns hung from trees. Gas-mantle lanterns, too, make attractive garden lights. Electric lighting, however, offers by far the greatest possibilities. Landscape lights are available both in 120-volt and in 12-volt systems. The latter are much lower in cost and are by far the more practical choice for a small garden. A 120-volt system should only be installed by a qualified electrician. The 12-volt systems, however, are manufactured for do-it-yourself installation. Such a system includes a transformer that lowers the potentially dangerous 110/120-volt current of a general-purpose domestic circuit to a safe 12 volts for use in the low-voltage system.

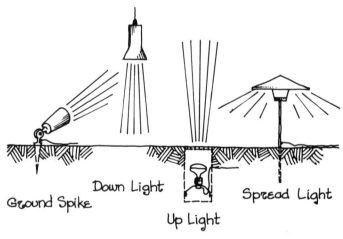

Down Light

Ground Spike

Up Light

Spread Light

These lights that throw a beam wherever you want it can be used for both safety and ornament. Up lights are also made in waterproof housings and can be used under water.

The variety of landscape lights on the market staggers the imagination. In terms of their effect on landscape elements and therefore the manner in which they should be used, they can be grouped

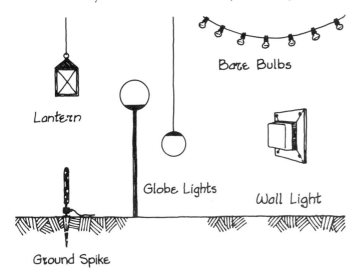

Lantern

Bare Bulbs

Globe Lights

Wall Light

Ground Spike

The lights that glow are used primarily for their luminous shape and to create interesting effects. However, they also cast considerable light on surrounding objects.

into two broad categories. The first have the following features in common: their light source is sufficiently strong to project light onto an area or object at which they are pointed. The light source therefore has to be concealed from direct view; in fact, it usually comes shielded on one or more sides. This category includes the familiar spotlights and floodlights. Since their light source is not intended for direct viewing and their primary function is to throw light, we will, for want of a better term and for purposes of explanation, call them "throw lights." There are "up lights" made to shine upward, and "down lights" made to shine down.

This is to differentiate them from what we might call "glow lights"—the other broad category of landscape lights. These are lights with a less intense or filtered light source that serves in itself as an object to be viewed. Shedding light onto areas or other objects is usually its secondary function. This category includes globe lights, cube lights and a variety of chandeliers, lanterns and bare-filament lamps. There are lights that do both, throw and glow—but for our purposes all lights will be treated as being predominantly either one or the other type.

The ways in which the two types of lights should be used is fairly obvious. Throw lights serve to highlight sculpture or foliage, to create deep, dramatic shadows or to bring out textures and to "wash" entire areas or walls with bright light. They come in a tremendous variety of configurations and sizes, mounted on posts, suitable for mounting on structures or on (or in) the ground. Up lights are made to be placed in wells to shine up into tree crowns or to be set in the bottom of a pool to illuminate a fountain. The most versatile arrangement is possible with lights mounted on spikes that are stuck into the ground. These are called ground-spike lights. The most important item to keep in mind about throw lights is to keep their light source out of the line of vision.

Glow lights, on the other hand, are meant to be seen. They can be used as lanterns, they can be placed to be reflected in water, to outline plant shapes in silhouette, to create light patterns and to create soft area lighting. These lights, too, are available in a great variety of shapes and sizes mounted on poles or ground spikes or sconces. They are available in systems of miniature bare-filament bulbs that can be draped over shrubs or small trees to outline their shape or in chains of larger bulbs that can be placed to festoon a trellis. In the form of globes or cubes or ornamental lamps they can be used as individual lanterns. Glow lights do not offend the eye and are easier to use well.

A question to consider is how will the light fixture look during the day? Both types of lights are available in forms that are in themselves ornamental, sculptural or otherwise pleasing in their appearance.

Lights with Water

In using lights with water, the water's reflective quality is important. Lights near water should always be placed with their reflected image in mind. Viewing a lighted harbor or boat landing from off-shore—first from afar, then closer in—provides an excellent opportunity to study the effects of light near water. Because of this reflective quality, lights near water should be predominantly glow lights. A mass of miniature incandescent bulbs, for example, in a low tree over a garden pool can bring to mind the reflection of a sky full of stars. A scintillating effect can be achieved with these lights over moving water. A low-intensity globe lantern suspended over water is reminiscent of the reflection of a full moon. Your own experience with light and water will suggest other possibilities.

Throw lights near water are best used to illuminate prominent shore features such as rocks or statuary that are enhanced by their reflection. Underwater up lights, too, are used successfully in elaborate fountains. Their use in small garden pools, however, is limited. Underwater lights can be successful in swimming pools but in shallower basins can interfere with the water's reflective quality.

A glow light hung above a pool is worthwhile for the reflection alone.

Lights with Plants

A great variety of lighting effects can be achieved with different plants. Both throw lights and glow lights have wide application in this area. The latter, however, are generally easier to use around plant material. A festive lacework of small incandescent bulbs can be placed to bring out a small tree's branching pattern or crown shape.

Low-intensity globe lanterns hung from branches can create a soft, evocative glow on a tree's foliage or can cast a swirling lacework of shadows on the lawn below.

Throw lights can produce stronger, more dramatic effects. They can be made to highlight tree trunks or specimen shrubs; set at the proper angle they can bring out interesting bark textures or patterns. Their placement, however, requires considerable care to keep the light source out of the beholder's eye. This can sometimes be done by hiding the light behind other plants or rocks. Up lights are frequently mounted in wells just below the surface of the soil and made to cast their light up into an overhead tree crown where it then filters upward through the foliage. This works especially well for tall, high-crowned trees seen from a distance. Down lights, too, can be used in tall trees. They can be suspended high in the

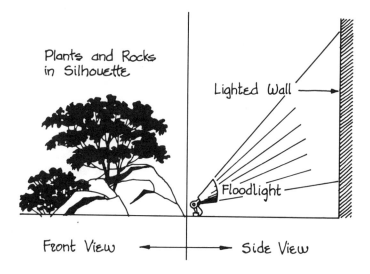

At night the shape of a plant can be dramatically accentuated by washing a wall or fence behind it with light. Even the most familiar plants will take on interesting new aspects.

crown to cast their light down along the trunk and to the base of the tree. A problem with that arrangement, however, is that when you stand under the tree and look up, you see something resembling an automobile headlight pointed at you. For this reason, really strong up or down lights had best be used in areas that would normally be viewed from a distance. The silhouette effect of closer plants, too, would thus come into full play.

A major shortcoming of many electric garden lighting systems is their limited color range. Foliage or floral color subtleties are frequently lost in artificial light. The emphasis in lighting plants, therefore, should be on the plant's configuration, pattern and texture rather than its coloration. Because of this limited color fidelity, the benefits in featuring flowering plants or flower beds with lights are relatively modest. One of the best ways to light flowers is to feature individual large blossoms with temporary spotlights.

Colored lights and colored lenses can be purchased for use in garden lights. Their color range, however, is minimal compared to white lights and their monochromatic effect on plants (not to mention people) can be downright ghastly. Though advertised as a vehicle of enchantment, their effect more often is transport into bizzarre fantasy.

Portable Spotlight

A narrow beam of light can be temporarily used to accentuate a single blossom or cluster of flowers.

Lights with Rocks

Lights used to illuminate rocks, sculpture or other structural or textural objects should be generally throw lights. The highlights and crisp shadows that they produce will enhance their three-dimensional qualities. Lights mounted low work well because the source is easily concealed and there is a potential for casting long and pronounced shadows onto nearby walls or slopes. Textures, too, are enhanced if the textured surface is washed by a low-angle floodlight.

Planning Your Garden Lights

Your first step in preparing the lighting layout should be to draw up a lighting effect plan. Establish your lighting objectives in program form. Answer questions such as: From where will the lighting be viewed? What areas or items should be highlighted, silhouetted or reflected? What areas will be islands of light in a field of darkness or vice versa? On the basis of these answers you can make your decisions of where throw lights would be appropriate or where you might prefer glow lights, what size and brightness they should be and how they will be mounted.

As a final step in planning your lighting system, you can experiment with flashlights or portable extension-cord lights to try out your ideas under field conditions. This will permit you to make a rough check on the practicality of your plan prior to investing in any fixtures.

As stated previously the most practical and least expensive type of garden lighting is a 12-volt system. Because of the relative safety of this low voltage, the 12-volt cables can be left to lie on the ground or can be buried without the expensive insulation or conduits required for the higher voltage systems. No wire splicing is required. Simple pin-type connectors do the job. A low voltage system thus has unlimited flexibility and can be even adapted to a changing or growing garden. Low voltage garden lighting systems are available at major garden stores or can be ordered through your hardware dealer.

After you have selected your light fixtures, add up the wattage of each to determine the total system load. This becomes the basis for selecting the transformer. The rating of the transformer should not be less than the total wattage. Transformers are available in weatherproof models suitable for outdoor mounting on building walls or other structures. They can be plugged into a regular outdoor electric outlet on a general purpose domestic 110/120-volt circuit. It is advisable to select equipment bearing the Underwriters Laboratory approved label. Any work that may be required on the 110/120-volt side of the transformer—such as extending existing lines, installing a new outlet or a switch for the outlet—should be done by a qualified electrician. For all other work, mounting the transformer, plugging it in, laying and connecting the 12-volt lines, placing or mounting the lights, simply follow the manufacturer's instructions.

A final point to remember: the purpose of garden light is *not* to turn night into day but to enhance the night by making your garden live in a vivid pattern of lights *and* shadows.

This high light covers a wide area and also reaches into the tree to illuminate the foliage and the flowers in their season.

9

A Swimming Pool
Is Water, Too

With the exception of the farm pond, the largest man-made container of water a home-owner is likely to be involved with is a swimming pool. While not meant to be essentially decorative, it is a welcome asset to the landscape if it can be more attractive than many backyard pools seem to be. Except for the house itself, a swimming pool is by far the largest element on the residential scene. It deserves the utmost attention as to location, design and surrounding amenities.

Where Should You Put It?

In positioning a pool on the site, assuming there is space enough to afford a choice, there are two different points of view.

One is to put it near the house for easiest possible access. Proximity probably does encourage more swimming and this argument takes on added validity if there is no budget for a pool-house and extra toilet facilities. If changing clothes is to be done in the house it is convenient to have the pool nearby. And if pool-side entertaining is to include food and drink, convenience dictates nearness to the kitchen.

The other concept is to put the pool well away from the house to reduce the impact of activity and noise (which can be considerable) and to avoid the glare of sun on the water. The degree to which all this affects life in the house depends on the relationship of the pool to the house and to the path of the sun.

A distant location usually calls for at least a minimal changing room, and preferably a pool-house. If entertaining is important, some kitchen and bar facilities are required. If one is to go that far, it may make sense to enlarge the space to accommodate a sleep-sofa which, in effect, creates a small guest house. Wiring and plumbing are also required. This approach to having a pool can be tempting—if it can be afforded.

It is easy to underestimate the total amount of space that will be required to accommodate a pool and all that it implies. The first consideration is accessibility for the truck that will bring the concrete for the pool. If there is clearance for this rig, there will be room for the back-hoe and other machines necessary to dig the hole. The amount of equipment used by pool contractors is astonishing—when it shows up in your back yard.

While you may choose the smallest pool recommended for swimming—about 14 by 34 feet —there must also be space for a paved walkway around the pool and a lounging area at one end. The minimum width for a walk is 3 feet, and it should really go all the way around. Add at least 3 feet more at the shallow end for sitting and 9 feet at the deep end for the diving board and the 3 feet needed for walking behind it.

The 14- by 35-foot area has now grown to 20 by 49 feet. If a fence is required, there should be at least 3 feet of clearance between it and the walk. The minimum is now 26 by 55 and we have not even considered a dressing room, and a place within this area will have to be found for the filter. On the basis of this simple example you can see why it is a good idea to do some careful measuring before you let the family get too excited about the beguiling prospect of having your own swimming pool.

Try to Hide the Filter

One of the least attractive aspects of a swimming pool, and one of the most necessary, is the filter.

With a little ingenuity, however, it need not be an eyesore. The small investment required to screen it from view is more than worth while. The improvement in the immediate environment of the pool is immediate.

When a pool is situated on a slope, the filter is usually installed at the low end, out of sight of the lounging area. This assumes that the lounging area is at the shallow end, which is usually best, for it is easier to oversee the small non-swimmers who play here and also puts the sitters and talkers well away from the splash and noise of divers at the deep end.

If the pool is on a flat site, screening the filter from view requires a little more imagination. If there is to be a pool-house, or even a simple changing room, it can often be placed where it can house, or at least screen out, the unsightly filtering equipment.

Failing this, a simple vine-covered trellis can quickly be made to do the job. It can also be done more subtly with a well-placed planting of evergreen shrubs and small trees, but it will take longer to accomplish.

In planning for the screening, also consider incorporating a place to store the pool vacuum, dip net and the other hardware that seems to become an unsightly part of the pool-side scene.

Most suburban communities require fences around the pool to prevent wandering persons, especially children, from falling in. By making the fence of board and at a height of at least 6 feet, privacy can also be attained. Your local lumber supply yard may have prefabricated sections of fence that are reasonably easy to install. A 6-foot fence is a workable wall and it doesn't take much more labor and material to extend it, in various ways, to provide screening and storage as suggested in the sketch below.

Plantings in front of the fence and vines that will grow on it are the time-honored methods of decoration and camouflage and are still hard to improve upon.

In most back yard installations the pool-side planting is remarkably unimaginative. The usual pattern is a stand of three white birches, a few flower beds and perhaps some pots of geraniums grouped in the neighborhood of the umbrella and lounging chairs. While such plantings are not bad, they are not related to the concept that a swimming pool is a man-made pond. Why not use some plants around the pool that are water-associated?

If the paving is brick, a 30-inch square could easily be opened up and the inside edge lined with 2 by 4's to hold the brick in place and the opening could then be planted with a good, sturdy, water-side plant such as equisetum. Or a plastic tub could be plunged in the opening and a planting

An existing fence, or building, can provide one wall and the needed support for a small storage place. A less ambitious project could include shelves only—without a roof.

of giant arrowhead, Egyptian paper plant, cattails or even a small lotus could be grown. An informal covering of river-washed stones between the edges of the tub and the brick would help to set off the plants. The rationale is obvious. If water plants are appropriate for a planting beside a pond, they are equally so for a pool-side display.

A stand of bamboo would be appealing, too, but it must be far enough from the pool to reduce the number of leaves that will inevitably blow into the water. In the chapter on plants that look well beside water (Part II, Chapter 1), you will find many good ideas for plantings that will support rather than deny the aquatic setting a swimming pool automatically creates. Even the plants in beds or containers that are normally used around a pool would be more appealing if at least one grouping consisted of such water-associated beauties as hosta, cardinal flower and water iris.

Plantings Are Important

It is expensive to make a swimming pool approximate the slow gentle work of nature instead of obviously revealing the quick brutal hand of man. But it is worth while if it can be afforded. Too many pools are all hard edges and glaring concrete. While a back yard installation is not the old swimming hole of song and story, and there are not many cascades and waterfalls in suburbia, there are some worthwhile ways to soften the obtrusive appearance of a pool in what may have been your rose garden.

A few well-placed boulders around the edge of the pool can be at least reminiscent of a mountain fastness. If the pool is on a slope, a small cascade of water recirculated from the pool can flow down over an artfully staged arrangement of rock. The sound of this water is appropriately refreshing beside a pool.

An irregular shape will also help to make the swimming pool appear to be more a natural occurrence than an intrusion on the landscape. A few low-growing evergreens and perhaps a large juniper or weeping hemlock hanging over the edge of the pool will make the whole more decorative. These slow-growing conifers will not appreciably dirty the pool. Once you decide to make the pool more natural in its appearance you will find ways to do so. A good landscape architect would be most helpful in this respect. In fact, if you can afford professional advice in siting and planning the entire installation, it is the best investment you could make.

A swimming pool of an irregular shape is a good choice for a natural setting. The curving lines seem to sit more comfortably here among the trees than would a rectangular pool. Shapes such as this are standard with many pool builders today. Notice that the trees are set well away from the pool to reduce the leaf-fall into the water.

The Naturalized
Swimming Pool

In some areas, the Northeast in particular, there are sites with natural outcroppings of rock. If you are fortunate enough to have one on your land and can incorporate it into the pool it will do wonders in naturalizing the setting. If it is in the wrong place and has to be blasted out, that can also be a nuisance and very expensive. In general it is better to reveal and enjoy rock outcroppings than to try to hide them.

The use of wood decking for the sitting area adjoining the pool also helps to reduce the hard look of an all-masonry installation. One deck, for a pool on a crowded site in the Chicago suburbs, was raised a few feet above the surface and cantilevered over the pool. This provided the much-needed lounging space and was high enough above the water so as not to interfere with swimming below.

A deck can be raised above grade to establish a welcome change of level, or it can be extended over a slope to provide living space without expensive retaining walls and fill. Splinters can be a hazard but there is no doubt that wood is attractive with water and a few shortcomings may well be overlooked.

A Real Problem—
the Above-Ground
Swimming Pool

Above-ground pools, with a plastic liner on a frame of wood, aluminum or steel, are the least expensive and by far the most difficult to integrate gracefully into the landscape. About the best one can hope for, if it is a full-sized pool, is to make panels of old-fashioned lattice, paint them the traditional green and put them all the way around the base of the pool to hide the unattractive framework. Some climbing vines on the trellis and groupings of evergreen shrubs in the foreground will also help tie the pool visually to the surrounding land.

One excellent idea for handling a small wading and swimming pool—about 10 feet in diameter

—was seen in a garden on Long Island. A round wood platform, about 6 feet larger in diameter than the pool, was raised 18 inches off the ground. The pool with an aluminum frame was centered on the platform, allowing 3 feet of walking space around the pool. Steps and a walkway connected the pool to the terrace which was just outside the kitchen door. The children could go from the house to the pool on a clean hard surface, which helped to keep the pool, as well as the kitchen floor, clean.

When the children outgrow the pool, it will be removed and the round raised deck will be a useful extension of the terrace. There was a landscape architect involved and this kind of multiple-use installation is typical of the kind of thinking one can expect from a good professional designer.

Placing a wading pool on a lawn will doubtless kill the grass underneath and the grass around the edges will be worn down; it is also impossible to trim the lawn right up to the edge of the pool; so it is a good idea to put a wading pool on a hard surface.

A Pool Does Not Take Care of Itself

Those who very much want to have a swimming pool, usually the younger members of the family, tend to believe that the necessary maintenance is minimal and can easily be done on a Saturday morning. The person who may be less enthusiastic about the prospect of a pool, usually the one who will be paying the bill, sees a future with little but constant cleaning, chemical mixing and plumbing repair. As is usually the case, the truth of the matter is somewhere between.

To keep the water sparkling clean and dependably free of infectious organisms, the water should be tested every day and corrective chemicals added if necessary. The test kits are quick and easy to use and the adding of the chemicals is not complicated. The test, however, must be made.

The static shape of a rectangular pool can often be enlivened by the shape, as well as the color and texture, of the surroundings. The pot plants are used for seasonal color.

A disinfectant must be used in the water to eliminate bacteria and algae which can discolor the water and cause unpleasant odors. Chlorine is the recommended chemical to use, and only testing with the kit can tell you whether or not there is enough in the pool to do the necessary job.

The dry forms of chlorine, such as calcium hypochlorite, or the newer organic chlorines are best to use. The liquid form, sodium hypochlorite, is a bleach and more corrosive than the powders.

Another daily test is for pH, to determine whether the water is acid, neutral or alkaline. pH is measured on a scale of 0 to 14 and 7 is neutral. A pool should be slightly alkaline (7.2 to 7.6) to utilize effectively the chlorine and reduce the incidence of metal and concrete corrosion caused by excess acidity. The usual test kits have colored indicator solutions and complete instructions as to what to do if the level is not what it should be.

The heart of the pool's cleaning system is the filter. The most popular systems use diatomaceous earth as a filtering medium. This inert substance, composed of the almost microscopic skeletons of sea-borne diatoms, is held in a container through which the pool water is pumped. It effectively screens out the impurities. The system is well proved but the filtering material can hold only so much foreign matter before it must be removed by backwashing (a rinsing process that takes a lot of water that must be disposed of somewhere). We won't go into the details of filter care here, but it is wise to be absolutely sure you know what must be done to keep the filter working well before you decide to have a pool.

There is considerable plumbing included in the filtering system as well as a pump and electrical connection to drive it. If you are a house owner you know that where there is mechanical equipment there is the possibility of breakdown and expensive repair.

If all of the above sounds discouraging, think of the traffic going to the beach and the crowds you will find when you get there!

This wealth of annuals and perennials is laid out in the shape of a curving stream bed and a small pool accentuates the illusion. But even a few flowers beside a placid pool reflected in its surface can be effective.

Part II

THE
BEAUTY OF
PLANTS

*Of every color of the rainbow—to have and to hold,
to use in drifts and beds, to create exclamation
points in the garden scheme and to cut and bring
indoors for beauty that man can never du-
plicate—these represent the glory of the flower.*

*There are sizes, shapes, fragrances and textures
to suit every mood and preference. What can match
the vibrant hues of the tulip? What fragrance can
equal that of the lilac and the rose? For purity of
line the water lily has no peer, and for sculptural
form what can match the camellia and the peony?*

*The foliage of the pine and hemlock, the glossy
privet and the leatherleaf viburnum describe an
incredible range of textures, and these are but a few
of what any gardener can easily have. The cost in
dollars is but a pittance. The true price for the
beauty of plants in your garden is imagination and
an understanding and fulfillment of their needs
—much of which can be learned herein.*

1

Plants That Look Well Beside Ponds and Streams

On the following pages are descriptions of trees and shrubs, ground covers and flowers, foliage, plants and ferns that are attractive and well suited to the conditions that prevail at the edges of ponds and streams.

Some of these are bog plants that will grow in wet soil and shallow water. Some will tolerate moisture in the root area at certain times in their growth cycle but not in others. Be sure you understand their requirements before you set them out.

In a natural pond, plants will find their way into the environment they must have. It may take years for them to get established and develop their character, but plants will eventually come up at the water's edge, and a pond or stream seems incomplete without them. In a pond of your own making, their effect can be attained immediately.

Plants add an upright accent to the flat edge where the water meets the land, and they serve to bridge the gap between the plants of dry land and those that grow entirely in the water. Their upright character is reflected in the water in varying forms, with the shifting light and moving surface, and their impact is thus doubled.

It is usually best to use small plants in clumps and drifts rather than in line along the edges. A circle of plants around the edge of a pond or pool, for example, tends to isolate it from its surroundings. The same plants used in attractively spaced groupings can relate the water to its surroundings instead of setting it apart.

Keep in mind the fact that many small aquatic and bog plants tend to spread. If they are used sparingly to begin with, less time will be required in cutting and pulling to keep them in bounds.

Shrubs are also best in masses. A group of three or five planted together to create a strong accent is more interesting than if strung out in a row along the edge. In the list of shrubs that follows some will actually take moist soil and others look particularly fine when planted near the water. You can have both if you know which is which.

Trees should be carefully sited. A tree is both a major feature in the landscape and a major investment. Once it is planted it is not easily moved to another place. Make sure you know where you want it when you set it out, and look at it not as the sapling it may be when you acquired it, but as the full-sized tree it will become. Remember that it will cast large shadows and, if deciduous, will drop bushels of leaves. Be sure the shade will be only where it is needed. If you have decided to establish a display of water lilies at one end of a pond or pool, you should not put a large tree where its shadow will cut off the sunlight the lilies must have. Leaves in the water are a problem, and trees should be planted back far enough from the edge so that not many of them fall in. If you know the prevailing winds in the area, perhaps the tree could be placed so that it will blow the leaves away from the water instead of toward it.

The following lists of plants recommended for use in the environs of a pond or pool are arranged approximately in the order in which they should be considered for planting. Certainly the trees should go in first, because they take much longer to get established and have such a critical effect on the rest of the plantings and the environment as a whole. The same is true, to a lesser degree, of the shrubs, which are listed next, on down to the small foliage plants and the ferns which will be used where needed for accent after the rest of the setting is pretty well established.

Trees to Consider for Pool-side Planting

Some trees look well beside a pool whether or not they grow well in moist places. The pine (*Pinus* in variety) is one. Japanese maple (*Acer palmatum*) is another and the flowering cherries (*Prunus serrulata, P. Sieboldi* and *P. subhirtella* and *P. yedoensis* and their varieties) are a third.

All these are widely used by the Japanese, and almost every Japanese garden has water in it. These plants have been associated with water for so long that they are as acceptable as the weeping willow, which is a native to moist places, as are most of those that follow:

Judas tree or Redbud *(Cercis canadensis)*. The magenta flowers in tight clusters appear before the leaves and cover the tree in a dazzling display. The color is on the garish side and does not combine well with other colors but does go with white. There is also a white variety, *C. c. Alba*. The spectacle of its flowers can be doubly enjoyed if planted so that it can be seen reflected in the water. Plant in light sandy soil where only the deeper roots will reach down to the water table.

Sweet-gum *(Liquidambar styraciflua)*. Surprisingly enough, this magnificent tree will tolerate some moisture in the root area. It is one of the finest of all trees for fall color and well worth planting where its autumn glory can be reflected in the water.

Weeping birch *(Betula pendula)*. The familiar snowy white bark of the birch is handsome wherever it is seen. It is especially attractive beside a brook or stream, perhaps because it reminds us of similar settings in the woods. The weeping form has the same waterfall branching as the willow, and the yellow-green catkins in the spring are an added delight.

Weeping willow *(Salix babylonica)*. This is the classic tree for water-side plantings. The long slender branches arch down and, if near the edge, will touch the water. The shape is attractive the year round but the tree is at its best in early spring when the buds appear as strands of golden beads along the thin arching branches. They swell and turn to foliage of chartreuse-green which clothes the tree completely. A well-grown willow will reach to 60 feet or so and should not be planted in a restricted place. The roots are invasive, so the tree should not be planted near water lines or drainage fields of tile. The golden willow *(S. vitellina)* has attractive golden bark that shows up particularly well in winter.

The cascading form of the weeping willow's foliage makes it one of the most attractive trees for stream- or pond-side planting.

Some Good Shrubs to Try

When you have decided where the trees will go, the shrubs are next to be considered. Here is some advice worth repeating: Plant shrubs in drifts (irregular groupings) and plant enough of one kind together to make a good showing. Do not line them up like ducks on the pond. Keep in mind that most shrubs are shallow-rooted, so that it is not a good idea to plant them near a stream that may flood and wash them out.

Arborvitae *(Thuja occidentalis* **and** *T. orientalis).* There are dozens of dwarf forms, many of which are somewhat stiff. This is, however, one of the few needle-leaf evergreens that does well in moist soil and as such is worthy of consideration.

Bog kalmia *(Kalmia polifolia).* Rather an erect, small, broadleafed evergreen shrub that grows to about 2 feet in height. Leaves are glossy green above and whitish below. The rounded clusters of small flowers range in color from pink to purple. This is a native that may be available from nurseries that deal in special plants.

Buttonbush *(Cephalanthus occidentalis).* The attractive foliage and the dense rounded heads of small tubular flowers in late summer make this a worthy shrub for boggy places. Grows to 12 feet or more. Deciduous.

Japanese pieris *(Pieris japonica).* One of the loveliest of all the shrubs. The open upright form is handsome, the foliage attractive and the graceful flower clusters are in constant change as the buds develop and the flowers and seeds form and fade. Grows to 8 feet or more. The broadleafed foliage is evergreen.

Japanese wisteria *(Wisteria floribunda).* With its 2-foot pendent panicles of purple or white flowers, this is one of the most dramatic of all vines. It is long-lived and vigorous and requires a sturdy support. In some cases it takes years for a wisteria to bloom but, even so, the foliage is decorative and the flowers worth waiting for. Deciduous.

Oak leaf hydrangea *(Hydrangea quercifolia)*. All hydrangeas will take moisture at the roots but the soil must be porous. This one was chosen to represent the group because it is not too large, grows to about 6 feet, and has lovely flowers and exceptionally handsome foliage. Deciduous.

Spice-bush *(Lindera benzoin)*. A tall deciduous shrub that displays its small green-yellow fragrant flowers early in the spring before the leaves come out. Showy scarlet berries appear in late summer and foliage turns yellow in the fall. It tends to re-seed itself prolifically but the seedlings can easily be pulled to keep it under control.

Swamp blueberry *(Vaccinium corymbosum)*. The blueberries all do best in moist peaty soil. They have handsome deep green foliage that turns to spectacular shades of red and orange in the fall. If conditions of sun are right, you may get the bonus of their tasty berries. Grows to about 12 feet in height. Deciduous.

Swamp dogwood or Tatarian dogwood *(Cornus alba)*. A handsome shrub in the spring with its array of white flowers on branches of showy red. It has a vigorous habit of growth and is not so tidy as the large rhododendrons and azaleas which also grow to about 10 feet. Deciduous.

Swamp honeysuckle *(Rhododendron viscosum)*. This late-flowering azalea blooms in July and is welcome in this season when few other water-side plants are in bloom. It grows to about 6 feet in height. This is not a bog plant and will not grow in stagnant water, but it will tolerate more moisture in the root area than most of the other azaleas.

Bamboo for a Strong Vertical Accent

A tall stand of swaying bamboo rustling in the wind beside a waterfall is a symphony of sight and sound and not beyond the range of anyone who lives where the winter temperature stays well above zero Fahrenheit.

There are many kinds and they are called by many names, including *Arundinaria, Bambusa, Dendrocalamus, Phyllostachys, Pseudosasa* and *Sasa*. Availability may be a problem, but if your nurseryman stocks bamboo it is worth considering for its dramatic effect. Bamboo is not a bog plant, but if the surface drainage is good it will thrive where there is moisture in the root area.

Bamboos constantly shed leaves and bark and should be planted well away from pools to keep the debris out of the water.

Bamboos have two kinds of root systems, clumping and running. Plantings of the clump type will spread but are not hard to keep in bounds. The running type is very difficult to control and can become a considerable nuisance. The roots run for many yards under ground and send up strong stalks where they will—even through an asphalt drive, or in a neighbor's lawn.

It is said that a circle of corrugated sheet metal driven vertically into the ground to enclose the root area will keep them from getting away but there are no guarantees.

All the hardiest bamboos, such as yellow grove *(Phyllostachys aurea)*, giant timber *(Phyllostachys bambusoides)*, sulphur *(Phyllostachys sulphurea)*, metake *(Pseudosasa japonica)* and palmate *(Sasa palmata)*, are of the running type. The hardiest ones of all, metake, sulphur and palmate, will withstand temperatures as low as 5° F.

The unmistakable character of bamboo.

None of the following are bog plants, but they will all grow in moist soil if it is porous and reasonably well drained. These ground covers are included here because they are among the most useful of all plants. If you have a slope near your pool a ground cover will clothe it fully and keep the soil from sluicing away in the rain. In narrow places between steppingstones or boulders the only practical plants to use are the ground covers. They need no trimming to keep them in bounds and they will find their way into the irregular spaces without guidance or control. There are many kinds to choose from, but these two evergreens are classics that have performed well enough in enough different places to have earned that designation. Once established they will crowd out other plants and weeds, but they must be weeded for a few seasons until they fill in.

Bugle-weed *(Ajuga reptans)*. The textured bronzy-green leaves lie quite flat to the ground in informal rosettes and are almost fully evergreen. In the spring attractive 6-inch spikes of blue, pink or white flowers rise above the leaves. Runners grow in all directions and root readily. This plant does well in sun or shade.

English ivy *(Hedera helix)*. There are many leaf forms of this species and new forms may develop on your own plants. The familiar rich green leaves, with veins of lighter color, grow on a flat plane and completely cover the ground. The ivy spreads by sending out long runners which then branch to the sides to fill in. It does best in a fairly rich soil and needs some winter shade.

Horsetail *(Equisetum hyemale)*. The tubular upright stalks are segmented like bamboo. It grows in wet places and almost any place else to a height of 4 feet. It is often seen running ram-

The Best All-Around Ground Covers

Good Grasses to Grow

pant along old railroad tracks and other out-of-the-way places. Because it spreads so readily it is best grown in a container. The stems are semi-translucent and are interesting seen against the light. It will survive a mild frost.

Arundo donax. A giant reed, rather like a tremendous cornstalk, that grows to about 15 feet during the summer. In the fall it ends the season with a handsome show of plumage at the top of the stems. It dies down in late fall, but, where frosts are light or non-existent, it will rise again in the spring. One of the most dramatic ornamental grasses.

Miscanthus sinensis. The long narrow green leaves have a center stripe of white that gives this grass a jaunty refreshing aspect. It grows to about 3 feet in height and in the fall the white flower plumes suffused with pink rise up from among the leaves. There is also a solid green form.

Pennisetum alopecuroides. A good ornamental grass with an outstanding feathery flower followed by a showy seed head in the fall. The texture of the flower is beautifully revealed when seen against the sunlight.

Wild rye or Lyme grass *(Elymus glaucus).* Lovely arching stems of narrow blue-green foliage make an attractive mound to 4 feet in height.

Use These Mostly for Their Bright Colors

If the foliage plants that thrive around the edges of a pond or pool are the staples, the highlights are provided by the plants that are noted for their flowers. They are appealing and one is tempted to use them all. Choose two or three of those you like best and plant them in small groupings or larger drifts rather than diffuse the overall effect with too few of too many different kinds.

Take a tip from the wild flowers, which naturally develop in sheets and drifts of color and are unsurpassed in their beauty.

A number of these flowers, in fact, have proved of such value in landscaping a pond, stream or bog that they are now being cultivated commercially and are available for transplanting in early spring and fall. Here are a few of the best to consider: wake robin *(Trillium grandiflorum, T. nivale and T. erectum)*; cardinal flower, which is described below; great lobelia *(L. siphilitica)*; and Solomon's seal *(Polygonatum biflorum)*.

Aruncus sylvester. This is a tall, astilbe-like plant but of much bolder proportions (see astilbe below). A plant of similar weight on the garden scene is the tall plume poppy *(Macleaya cordata* which is often listed as *Bocconia cordata)*. This plant needs plenty of room and will use every inch it gets—and then some.

Astilbe. Here is a plant that is readily available, grows quickly, does well in sun and shade and is remarkably handsome from spring until late fall. It has showy clusters of upright feathery flowers in white, pink or red. It blooms in summer and the flowers are followed by seed heads that are almost equally attractive. The red stems and foliage tinged with red give it further distinction. There are a number of species and varieties of different size. The average height is 3 or 4 feet.

Bergenia cordifolia. Perhaps better known for its rounded deep green foliage, one should not overlook the handsome purple flowers in early spring that are carried well above the leaves. It is not a bog plant but makes a good ground cover, grows to about a foot in height, in moist places, in sun or shade.

Cardinal flower *(Lobelia cardinalis)*. The striking flowers of deep cardinal red are borne on strong, 2-foot spikes in late summer and early fall. It looks best when planted in clusters. The foliage of this useful perennial is a refreshing deep green.

Day lilies (*Hemerocallis* **in variety**). Sturdy clusters of upright foliage make a handsome show from spring until fall. The flowers, which bloom from mid-summer until fall, develop in early morning and fade at night, a habit that gives them their common name. New flowers are continually coming on and if day lilies are grown in moist rich soil in a sunny place, they provide a continuous display of bloom in their season. The more light the better, but they will flower with a minimum of four hours of sun a day.

Ligularia clivorum **var.** *Desdemona*. The flowers look rather like those of the black-eyed Susan.

All the plants, including the cardinal flower (Lobelia cardinalis) *shown here in bloom, were brought in by the stream at high water.*

Foliage is bold and round. Grows to about 30 inches in height.

Marsh marigold *(Caltha palustris)*. This is a lovely little plant that makes a compact rounded cluster of foliage topped in spring with a generous sprinkling of bright buttercup-yellow flowers. It grows to about 18 inches in height.

Primrose *(Primula pulverulenta* and *P. bulleyana)*. These are two of the best of the Asiatic candelabra types. The striking flowers stand straight and tall, rising from a handsome cluster of heavily textured medium green leaves. The petals are carried at intervals in circlets around the stem. There are selected hybrids in a good range of warm glowing colors. *Primula Sieboldi japonica* is another good primrose to consider.

Sweet flag *(Acorus calamus)*. Broad dark green leaves grow 3 to 4 feet in height. Small white to green flowers are borne on a 2-inch spike at the end of a long thin stem. It has a sweet scent, particularly when the leaves are crushed or bruised.

Water canna *(Thalia dealbata)*. Not hardy where the temperature reaches freezing point in the winter, but worth while wherever it can be grown. A white powder on the 8-inch ribbed leaves gives them a distinctive blue-green appearance. The pyramidal clusters of purple flowers are carried on curving stems in late summer and early fall. It grows 3 to 4 feet in height, with the roots under water at the edge of a pond or submerged in a pot of soil. Can be moved indoors and carried over the winter as a house plant.

Water plantain *(Alisma plantago—agratica)*. The pointed leaves are heavily ribbed. The arching stems grow to about 3 feet in height. Its glory is the display of tiny pale pink flowers on a rounded airy structure of thin stems. It grows well in shallow water.

Small and Choice But Not So Showy

The following few are not so showy as those listed above, but they are engaging small plants worthy of attention. Pay heed to their requirements for moisture. They vary considerably.

Forget-me-not *(Myosotis scorpioides)*. This is a familiar favorite, with flowers of bright blue. It can be grown in a shady place and started from seed planted in moist loam.

Hepatica *(H. americana)*. An early bloomer. The flowers appear in the spring when little else is in color, are star-shaped and may be white or blue or purple-blue. The foliage has three distinctive lobes and is carried on hairy stems. It does best in full shade where the soil is dependably moist but not soaked.

Trout lily *(Erythronium americanum)*. Here is a native American plant that tends to colonize and spread in moist, but not water-logged, soil. It has brown-mottled pointed leaves 6 to 10 inches in length. The small lily-shaped flowers are produced only after the planting is well established.

Water arum *(Calla palustris)*. This flower is similar to the calla lily. It has the typical flowers in the shape of a sheath around a flower spike. It blooms in June and July, and you may see snails on the stems at that time. They do no harm and are fulfilling the useful function of fertilizing the flowers. Leaves are bright green and heart-shaped. This is a true bog plant that thrives with its roots in the mud.

Water poppy *(Hydrocleys nymphoides)*. The bright yellow, poppy-like flowers appear among handsome, smooth-edged, oval leaves. It grows in 2 to 4 inches of water. It also grows in deeper water and, when rooted, develops new plants that break loose and float free. It makes an attractive plant to use in shallow containers.

The iris, with its upright foliage ranging in width from grasslike to swordlike, and flowers with interesting shapes and clear colors, is among the most attractive plants to use beside a pool or stream.

The familiar tall bearded iris and the bulbous iris require soil with good drainage and in a water-garden setting could be grown only in raised beds.

There are, however, some charming irises smaller than the bearded type that do well in damp or swampy places and are appropriate to consider here. They require soil on the slightly acid side, but this should be no problem. Except in alkaline soils the required acidity can usually be maintained by feeding twice a year with an acid fertilizer. As with all of the beardless irises, these can be propagated by division after flowering in the fall, or before growth begins in the spring.

Some Irises That Will Grow in Moist Places

Just a gallon or two of water can brighten any scene, as does this bird-bath in a bed of iris.

The Japanese iris is a charming plant and has flowers of good size in proportion to the foliage. The colors are in the white to lavender, purple and pink range. Named hybrids of most of these species are available from iris growers.

I. kaempferi. This fine Japanese species blooms in mid to late summer. It requires moisture around the roots in spring and summer, but the root area should be well drained in winter. Sometimes a flow of water can be diverted by a few well-placed scoops with a shovel, or the iris can be grown in a box with a bottom of heavy wire and raised up above the moist soil area for the winter season. The foliage grows to a height of 2 to 3 feet.

I. laevigata. This form has narrower leaves than *I. kaempferi* and grows to about 2 feet in height. The flowers are a lovely shade of blue. It is by nature a bog plant and will thrive with moisture in the root area the year round.

You Can Grow Them Almost Anywhere

There are three species of iris that grow in the bogs and bayous of Louisiana. The names are *Iris foliosa, I. fulva* and *I. giganticaerulea*. These and the hybrids that have been developed from them are naturals for touches of color in moist places. The color range is from white and yellow to pink, red, purple and blue. They grow from 2 to 3 feet in height.

I. pallida. While this lovely plant with lavender bloom is not usually found in wet areas, it is obligingly tolerant of dampness, and, in view of its variegated foliage, makes a striking accent plant whether in or out of flower.

Siberian iris (*I. sibirica*). This species will grow in moist soil or shallow water. The narrow grasslike leaves are deep green and the flowers are white or blue. The white variety, Snow Queen, is an excellent choice. This iris grows to about 2 feet in height.

Water iris. There are two species called by this name. Both are semi-aquatic and will grow in shallow, but not stagnant, water.

I. versicolor. This one has dense clusters of upright foliage. The flowers are purple to blue, and the plant grows to 2 feet or more.

Yellow flag (*I. pseudacorus*). The flowers are yellow and are sometimes veined with purple. It grows to about 3 feet.

Yellow iris (*I. ochroleuca* or *I. orientalis*). These are two separate species that are sometimes confused in the trade. Only one is yellow. *I. ochroleuca* has white to yellow flowers and grows to about 3 feet. *I. orientalis* grows to 2 feet or less and has white to purple flowers.

Dwarf iris (*I. pumila*). This is an iris that calls for dry soil on the alkaline side and is by no means a moisture-loving, water-side plant. It is, however, such an attractive plant and its small tufts of swordlike leaves look so at home by the water that it is often worth growing in a tub of specially prepared soil. It flowers in early spring and grows to about 6 inches in height. *I. p. caerulea* is a lovely blue; *excelsa* is an attractive yellow.

2

Plants That Grow in the Water

When you see a lake of crystal clear water with plants growing around the edge, under the water and on the surface and with fish swimming about and snails browsing on the bottom, you are seeing a body of water in an admirable state of biological balance.

It is a balance that can be attained in a pool or pond in your own back yard if you understand the principles involved. The plants and the fish are the critical factors. Fish take up oxygen from the water and give off carbon dioxide. Plants take up carbon dioxide from the water and release oxygen. Because the plants and the fish each give off something the other needs, they both grow better when they are together than they do separately. The fish also eat mosquito larvae and other bits and pieces of matter in the pool. The scavengers such as snails clean up the debris that sifts to the bottom.

When the proper number and kind of plants are brought together a natural balance will be established and the pool will be a joy to behold. If there are too many plants, or if the soil in the bottom of the pool or in the boxes that hold the water plants has too much organic matter, the water can become cloudy and unpleasant odors may develop. It is not difficult to balance a pool but the natural laws must be observed. Organic matter in the soil, such as peat moss, compost or manure creates unpleasant gasses as it decomposes. To lighten the texture of underwater soil, use sand, not organic matter.

There should be an inch or so of coarse sand on the bottom of the pool and on top of the soil in any planting tubs and pots that are submerged. This will keep the fish from roiling the mud at the bottom and clouding the water. All plants give off some oxygen but there are a few that are particularly efficient. These are called oxygenators by the suppliers. Some of them will grow by simply floating on the water, but the most efficient oxygen producers are those that are rooted in the soil, either on the bottom of the pool or in pots set on the bottom. When the light hits the plants right, you can see on the stems and leaves the bubbles of air that break away and rise to the surface.

If you don't intend to plant them, wrap a piece of plastic-covered wire around the base of the stems and drop it in the pool. The weight will keep it in the necessary upright position.

The following are marsh plants that will grow in pots with 4 to 6 inches of water above the soil line. And don't forget the topping of sand to hold the soil in place.

Ludwigia. This popular plant has rounded flat leaves on stems that rise upright to the surface. The green leaves turn to a coppery color on top when exposed to the sun, and a bright red on the undersides.

Parrots feather or water milfoil *(Myriophyllum proserpinacoides).* The light green whorls of plumelike foliage rise above the surface of the water for a decorative point of interest.

Primrose creeper *(Jussiaea repens).* The sinuous stems bear bright green leaves and small primroselike flowers.

**Plants That
Specialize in
Producing Oxygen**

The following plants do best when grown in deep water, from 16 to 24 inches. They are the most efficient oxygen producers and also provide spawning places for the fish.

Anacharis. The narrow deep green leaves are carried in whorls on long stems that rise gracefully from the bottom. The plants spread by runners when planted on the bottom of the pool and the old growth tends to turn yellow. When this occurs, the old sections should be pinched off and removed.

Cabomba. A plant with bright green finely cut fan-shaped leaves on a slender stem. All of its growth is underwater. It is also used frequently in aquariums. Fish may eat some of the new foliage but this will not damage the plant.

Water milfoil *(Myriophyllum verticillatum).* This is similar to Cabomba but has more elegant fanlike sprays of foliage on the curving stem.

Sagittaria. A handsome plant that grows on the bottom with graceful arching sword-shaped leaves of dark green. In shallower water where the stems rise above the surface, it may produce a small white flower and much longer arrow-shaped leaves. Miniature sagittaria is essentially the same plant only smaller in scale with narrower leaves. It does best if planted under 12 to 14 inches of water.

Eel grass *(Vallisneria spiralis).* It has long narrow upright grasslike leaves of a light, almost translucent green that move gently with the current. It is a neat plant that does not spread as readily as most of the other oxygenators. It sometimes bears a small white flower on the surface of the water.

The ability of these plants to grow without soil is such that many of them become invasive floating weeds when they are not kept under control. They grow even more robustly when rooted in the soil—with the leaves above water. The water hyacinth is notorious for its vigor. In warm waters it has clogged canals and become a hazard to navigation. It is considered so dangerous in this regard that it is not allowed to be shipped in interstate commerce. You can, however, often find it locally in a nursery that handles water plants. It is an attractive aquatic and not difficult to control in small areas. This is true of all the fast-spreading floating plants. When there are too many on the surface, just scoop them up and throw them away.

There are a variety of floating plants available. They are usually grown as annuals, and replaced every year. Some may live longer but it's not a major loss if they don't. None of them are expensive. Those mentioned here are among the most popular but others are available. They all serve the same purpose, which is to provide the shade necessary to inhibit the growth of algae and root areas underwater, which fish use for spawning and protective cover. Many of them are quite beautiful as plants and there is something fascinating about plants that require no soil to grow in.

Azolla caroliniana. A fast-spreading plant with tiny notched leaves. It has an attractive mosslike appearance but can become a pest unless kept under control. It is best to use in small areas where control is relatively easy. The dark green color that appears in shade turns to bronzy-green in the sun.

Salvinia auriculata. The tiny heart-shaped leaves have an interesting hairy texture. It spreads too fast to recommend for pools without goldfish. The fish help keep it under control by eating the new

Plants That Live on Air and Water

tender roots. They may also occasionally eliminate it altogether.

Water chestnut *(Trapa natans)*. Another floater with tiny leaves. These are triangular and toothed, about 4 inches across. The cluster is kept afloat by the hollow stems.

Water fern *(Ceratopteris thalictroides)*. This plant has clusters of dark green fluted and veined foliage, lettucelike in character. It grows to a foot across and rises a foot above the water. New plants develop at the edge of the leaves and break off and float away to start on their own.

Water hyacinth *(Eichhornia crassipes)*. The rounded hollow stems bear rounded arched and pointed leaves. It has attractive upright clusters of multi-petaled violet to lavender flowers with yellow centers. The flower clusters are much smaller than those of the unrelated Dutch hyacinth for which it is named. The species *E. azurea* has purple to blue flowers. It also spreads vigorously but does not have the air-filled stems of the other one. It spreads by means of runners on the surface of the water.

Water lettuce or shell flower *(Pistia stratiotes)*. The thick heavily veined leaves are a fresh light green and grow in rosettes up to 6 inches across. The long feathery roots will readily grow in the soil when grounded.

*Here is a handsome array of textures with the sword-
like leaves of the iris and the linear fern and dwarf bamboo
foliage combined with a dense flotilla of lily pads.*

*The contrast of textures in the different plants—lilies, iris,
azalea, and skunk cabbage—and some fine old weathered
rocks setting off the saucer shapes of the lily pads, is well
planned here.*

3

Lilies and Lotus— Brightest Jewels in a Liquid Setting

Why do these plants have such undeniable appeal? Why does their image stay in our minds? Upon seeing other flowers in the garden, we often fail to match the name to the bloom or the foliage. But the water lily and the lotus, once seen, are not to be forgotten.

Could it be the intensity of their color, the clean crisp form, the shape—so seemingly simple but complex upon examination? Or is it the foliage? The water lily has leaves gracefully floating and moored to the root with a life line receding mysteriously into the depths. The lotus has leaves like parasols. Neither is likely to be confused with any other plant. Their attraction includes the foregoing attributes as well as the environment in which they grow. No doubt about it, there is nothing to compare to these bright jewels that glow in their watery setting.

Both water lilies and the lotus can be grown in a pool, of course, but also in a tub set into the ground or on the surface. There are miniatures with 2-inch flowers that require no more than 4 square feet of area and a depth of 6 inches. Some of the smallest will grow in a 12-inch bowl. At the other end of the scale, there are lotus with leaves more than 2 feet across, with flowers above these, the whole rising to 6 or 8 feet.

There are lilies of every color. Some bloom in

the daytime and some at night. With a little thoughtful planning you can have water lilies in bloom around the clock. For all their beauty they have a practical side as well. These lilies provide one of the easiest ways to have color in the garden. No cultivating is required, and there is little need for weeding, thinning or pruning. Very few pests attack them. They need no extra watering; and feeding, which they do need, is easy to accomplish.

The Two Kinds

The hardy lilies, the species of which are native to America and Europe, have been extensively hybridized. The foliage is oval to heart-shaped with clean crisp edges. There are hundreds of available varieties (and species) in almost every color but blue. Some open with one color and slowly change color on succeeding days. The hardy kinds are all day-bloomers that open in the early morning and close in the late afternoon. The flowers of most of the hardies float on the water, but there are some that carry the flowers above the water on short stems. In most cases the flower will bloom for three successive days, and the opening and closing process, which is interesting to observe, takes about an hour. They will thrive and come up year after year wherever the roots can be kept from freezing.

The tropical lilies are the other kind. In their native state they grow in Mexico, South America, Africa and India, and they, too, have been propagated to produce a wide range of colors. Pink, red, white and yellow are favorite colors, and the purples and blues are outstanding. The tropicals are larger in both foliage and flower, and the leaves of most are fluted or scalloped. Because they are native to warm climates, they are tender and the roots usually die if touched by frost. In climates warm enough for citrus fruits to be grown commercially, many of the tropicals will carry on from year to year. But where frost is expected, they should be considered annuals and new plants set out every year. They are not inexpensive, but there is nothing to compare with their effect in the garden.

Among the tropicals there are both day-bloomers and night-bloomers. Most of those that flower by day, and many that bloom at night, are fragrant. They have a scent rather like that of tropical fruits, quite unlike that of any other flower. The day-bloomers open early in the morning and close late in the afternoon. A given flower on a healthy plant will continue to bloom for about five days. In this group are the blue and purple varieties, as well as a good choice of other colors. Among the night-bloomers, which open about dusk and stay open until about noon the following day, white is the predominant color. The

One or two choice lilies grown in a well-defined pool can be the focal point of an entire garden.

flowers of tropicals are borne well above the water on strong stems which make them ideal for cutting to bring into the house. When fully open, bring them in and put them in water.

Both kinds belong to the same genus, *Nymphaea*. There are about 40 species, and there is considerable confusion as to their botanical names. In the catalogs they are clearly listed as hardy or tropical, day- or night-blooming, so the niceties of nomenclature are not important. It is worth while, however, to know the names of three men who have made outstanding contributions to the development of the water lily, and thus to the color you can have in your garden.

Working in his garden in southern France with various species of hardy lilies around the turn of the century, M. Bory Latour Marliac developed a great number of varieties that are still among the finest of their kind. More recently, Dr. George H. Pring of the Missouri Botanical Gardens in St. Louis has made many magnificent contributions to the development of the tropical kinds. Another person who has earned a good reputation working with the tropical kinds is Martin E. Randig. Their names, on varieties you will see listed in the catalogs, are an assurance of dependable plant characteristics.

Be Sure There Is Space Enough

The first requirement is space enough to grow the plants well. There must be sufficient water area for the leaves to spread out and for the plant to develop to its fullest capacity. From the horticultural point of view, one could grow as many plants as the water area will accommodate, but from the design point of view it is better to have areas of open water between the plants to set them off and to reflect the clouds and changes of light in the sky. If the surface is filled with foliage, you will miss the pleasure of seeing the fish that every pool should have.

For the best effect, less than half the surface of the water should be covered with plants. Some are vigorous growers that will cover up to 12 square feet of water surface (say 3 by 4 feet). A medium-sized plant will cover about 10 feet, and the smaller kinds, except for the pygmy types, take about 4 square feet. In a 6- by 9-foot pool, with 54 square feet of surface, no more than 25 feet should be given over to plants. Most catalogs give some indication as to the size of the plants. The tropicals, as mentioned above, are larger in every way than the hardies.

They All Need Sun and Rich Soil

No matter how much you wish it were otherwise, water lilies and lotus will not flower without long hours of sunlight—the more sun the better. This applies to all kinds: day-bloomers, night-bloomers, hardies and tropicals. Even the few that may be listed in catalogs as tolerating some shade will produce larger leaves and larger flowers if they have sun from early morning until late in the afternoon.

If you want to have trees as a background planting, and there is nothing lovelier than a willow or weeping birch by the water, put them on the north side and well away from the edge of the water where they will not cast a shadow on it.

Where some shade is unavoidable and you want to try them anyway, plant the lilies with about one-third less water above the roots than the standard recommendations specify in the planting information that follows.

The large area of foliage and the number of flowers produced by each plant are sure indications of their need for good rich soil—and for supplementary plant food. The best soil is heavy garden loam with some clay content. Sandy soils will not do.

Well-rotted cow manure is the ideal fertilizer but impossible for most gardeners to get. Next best are the commercial plant foods sold by the nurseries that deal in aquatics. It is also recommended that a couple of handfuls of bone meal be included in each planting. If the fertilizer is added only to the bottom 2 or 3 inches of soil, it will be where the roots can get to it readily.

Do not use peat, compost, or other organic materials to enrich the soil, and do not use garden soil that has such ingredients. These materials will continue to decompose and give off gasses that cloud the water and can harm the fish. If you see gas bubbles rising from the root area, such decomposition is probably the cause.

Planting in Boxes Is Best

Planting in tubs and boxes is a useful practice for all plants that require a special kind of soil, and there are other good reasons for growing water lilies in containers. It is much easier to plant them in boxes and lower them into the pool than to plant directly in the soil on the bottom—and, of course, it's the only way to plant if the pool has a bottom of masonry or wood. The quantity of water above the soil is an important factor in growing water lilies. Roots planted in boxes can be set on bricks or concrete blocks and raised and lowered as required to maintain the proper water level. The process of lifting and replanting is also simplified when the roots are in containers. The cleaning of the pool, which should be done every spring, is much easier if all the plants can be lifted out in their boxes.

The pool should be at least 2 feet deep to accommodate a foot of soil in the container and a foot of water over the roots.

Plastic containers of the sizes recommended for various kinds of lilies are available from the nurseries that handle aquatics. They also have wooden tubs and boxes for sale. You can easily make your own boxes as shown in the drawing at the right.

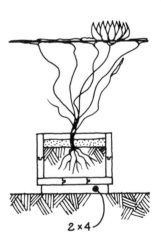

2 x 4

A simple planting box like this should be 12 inches deep inside and 18 to 24 inches square outside.

The containers for the equisetum in the foreground and the miniature papyrus show under the water but they are neatly made and do not detract from the overall setting.

Planting the Hardy Kinds

You can plant the hardy water lilies as soon as the water is dependably warm. In zone 5 on the U.S.D.A. climate zone map (page 158) this will usually be mid-April or early May. In areas north of this zone it may be a few weeks later, and in those south of it a few weeks earlier.

Where there is little danger of frost, as in zones 9 and 10, the roots can be planted as early as February. If you have ordered by mail, the dealer will decide, on the basis of experience, when it is safe to send your lilies. Fill the pool a week or so before the plants are expected so that the water will have reached its natural outdoor temperature.

You can plant the hardy lilies in dry soil and simply set the container in the pool, but there will be less shock and the probability of more immediate initial growth if you submerge the soil-filled container in the pool for a few days before the plants are put in. The temperature all through the soil will then be adjusted to that of the water.

The roots will come to you moist and carefully wrapped. It is best to plant them immediately. If this is not possible, open the package, put it in a cool shady place, cover with wet burlap and keep it moist until the moment you plant. Any dryness will impede growth. The roots, or rhizomes, will come with obvious growing points, and some may have stems and leaves showing. Some of the rhizomes are horizontal, with the new growth developing along their length. Others, the Marliac Hybrids in particular, are vertical in shape, with the growth points on top of the root mass.

For each kind the planting principle is the same. Set the rootstock so that it is covered with no more than an inch of soil and so the growing points stand well above the surface of the soil. Put a flat stone over the root to hold it firmly into the soil. Then cover the entire soil area with at least an inch of sand or fine gravel. This will keep fish from disturbing the soil and clouding the water. Take the utmost care so as not to touch the growing tips. They are sensitive and easily damaged.

As soon as a box is planted, lower it gently into the pool. If it is submerged so that the soil has no more than 2 feet of water over it, the container can safely be set at that depth on the bottom or raised up on blocks or brick. If the pool is 3 or 4 feet deep (the hardy lilies will grow successfully at these depths), the water at the bottom of the pool is colder, and they should be lowered about a foot a week to reduce the shock of sudden temperature change.

If you are filling a new pool that is more than 2 feet deep, set the plant container into the tempered water at a level that will provide a foot of water above the soil. Add a little water every few days to fill the pool.

Winter Protection

The hardy lilies (and the goldfish) will survive the winter if the water or the soil they are in does not freeze. If, for example, you live where the ice will not be more than a foot thick, you can safely overwinter the roots in containers set on the bottom of a pool 3 feet deep. This is a good reason for having a deeper pool in the colder climates. The depth of the ice can be reduced, and freezing often prevented completely, by insulating the pool with a covering of boards—leaving a few cracks for air—and a covering of straw or leaves with plastic netting or chicken wire laid over the pile and staked down to keep the insulation from blowing away.

If there are fish in the pool, the ice should be broken frequently to admit oxygen. Float a rubber ball or chunk of log in the pool and press it gently with the foot to keep an open spot in the ice. The gentle breaking prevents shock which could kill the fish. It also prevents the build-up of pressure that can crack a pool and cause it to leak.

If the pool is so shallow that there is danger of frost reaching the roots in their container, it should be drained and filled with leaves heaped up and held in place as suggested above. Push the containers into the sunniest spot in the pool.

In the spring when all danger of frost is past, the leaves can be removed and the pool cleaned and made ready to be refilled.

If you would rather lift the roots, wash them well and store them in a cool place safe from freezing in boxes of moist sand. The sand, however, must be kept moist throughout the winter. The container with roots in place can also be moved to a frost-free place and kept moist for winter storage.

Divide the Hardy Lilies Every Few Years

Unless the hardy lilies are taken up and divided every three or four years, they will show signs of deterioration. The foliage may lose color and the flowers diminish in size and number. Most growers recommend lifting and dividing the roots in the spring, but it can also be done in the fall. Bring the containers to the surface, lift out the roots and wash them off to reveal the growing points clearly. Cut away and discard the obviously old and woody parts. Cut the active part of the rootstock into sections that have two or three eyes or sprouted growing points. These sections can be planted as they were originally. The same process applies to the Marliac types, except that you cut vertically down between the growing points, leaving two or three on each new section. The extra pieces can be given away or used to start other containers of plants. Observe the same precautions you did with plants from the nursery. Do not touch the growing points and keep the roots moist until replanted.

Planting in a Deep Pond

Most of the hardy lilies, and the *odorata* species in particular, can be grown in a pond, lake or slow-moving section of a stream in water as deep as 10 feet or so. Some mail-order catalogs list special collections recommended for deep water. The Marliac hybrids are probably the best to use because they tend to spread less vigorously.

An easy way to plant is to fill a lightweight wooden container, such as a half-bushel peach basket, with soil and plant as recommended above. Use a rope to lower basket and all into the pond where you want the lilies to grow. Don't forget the flat rock to hold the root in place until the plant becomes established.

The basket will disintegrate as the roots establish themselves in the bottom. Do not plant too many to begin with because even the best-behaved kinds will increase in number.

If you can control the water level in the pond, you might want to lower it to a foot or so, plant the roots and gradually raise the level back to normal as the lilies grow. Or you can simply set the plants at the 2-foot depth in the shallows around the pool. To plant, push a spade into the soil at an angle, pry up the soil, set the rootstock in the open slit and press down firmly. Keep the growing points facing up and be careful not to touch them.

As mentioned above, the flowers of the tropicals are larger—up to 10 inches across—usually fragrant and carried well above the water. If you want flowers in the blue and purple range, you can get them only with the day-blooming tropicals.

With zone 5 on the U.S.D.A. climate map used for reference, as was done with the hardy lilies, the usual planting time will be mid-May or early June, earlier in gardens in the South and later in gardens in the North. Only in zones 9 and 10, where oranges and lemons grow, can they be left in the pool for the winter. In all other areas it is best to consider tropicals as annuals and enjoy them as such. Although they are started later in the year than the hardy kinds, they will usually be well into growth when you get them. They can also last longer in the fall. They do not go dormant until October, and if there is no frost they can bloom until then. Where the growing season is long enough, you can get two months more bloom time from the tropicals than from the hardies.

How to Plant the Tropicals

Because they are larger and grow more vigorously, the tropicals need more soil in the root area and more fertilizer. Instead of a container that will hold the bushel of soil recommended for the hardies, give the tropicals at least a bushel and a half of soil. A box a foot-and-a-half square and a foot deep will suffice. As for pool area, allow a surface of about 5 square feet (30 inches by 30 inches) for each tropical plant. Remember, it is best not to cover more than half the surface of the water with flowers and foliage.

Fill the planting pool with water at least two weeks before you expect to plant. This will give the water time to warm to the required temperature of 70° F. or over. At water temperatures under 70°, tropical lilies may go dormant.

The roots of the tropical plants are tuberous, rather like small sweet potatoes or yams, as compared to the rhizomes of the hardy kinds. Put the soil-filled planting containers in the water a few days before you get the roots. Plant them immediately upon arrival. Make a depression in the soil in the middle of the container and gently push the root mass down into it. Press soil gently and firmly over the roots so it barely covers them. Do not, under any circumstance, cover the crown of the plant with soil. A flat stone set over the roots to hold them down is also a good practice for the tropicals, and cover the soil area with an inch of sand to keep fish from disturbing.

These are the showy tropical lilies that bloom at night and carry their colorful flowers above the water.

As soon as the roots are planted, set the container in the water, leaving about 4 inches over the surface of the soil. Untangle the foliage, flowers and buds so that they flow nicely on the water. When the plants have grown for a few weeks, turn, or remove, the bricks on which the container is set to increase the depth of water above the soil to about 6 inches. This is the recommended depth for tropical lilies, although they can be submerged to 10 or 12 inches. They do better in warm water, and it is warmest near the surface. This would suggest that they should be planted more shallowly in cooler climates and in places where there may be some shade.

When the plants die back in the fall, clear out all the dead and dying foliage. The containers can be left in the pool until spring when it is time for the annual cleanup, which is also the time to replace the soil and get ready to plant the display of tropicals for the coming year.

New Plants That Start by Themselves

Some of the day-blooming tropicals are viviparous which means they have the interesting characteristic of developing entire new plants on the leaves of the old. The new plant, a perfect miniature of the parent, begins as a lump at the base of the leaf where it joins the stem. The minute stems and leaves break through and begin to grow. In some cases, a tiny flower will develop.

The new plants can be easily rooted. Separate the leaf from the stem and lay it flat on the surface of saturated soil in a flower pot or other container large enough to accommodate the leaf. The container must have openings to let water in and keep the soil saturated. Hold the leaf in place with toothpicks set in at an angle around the edge. If you use a flower pot or, better yet, the shallower bulb pan, put it in a saucer that can be kept filled with water which, in turn, will keep the soil in the pot constantly moist by capillary action. Or you can put the container rim-deep in the pool. The sunnier the location the better. When the parent leaf has decomposed and the new plant is well established on its own, it can be planted in a full-sized container, put into the pool and lowered gradually as the stems grow longer. The new plant may have more than one leaf cluster. If so, the plants should be carefully separated with a sharp knife and planted individually. Otherwise they will be too crowded to develop fully. These piggy-back plants are more of a curiosity than an addition to the beauty of the lily. If you think that handling the new plants will be more trouble than they are worth, avoid buying this type. In the catalogs they are identified as viviparous or leaf-propagating plants.

Star Lilies

The name derives from the clearly defined symmetrical pattern of the narrow, pointed flower petals. The star lilies bloom abundantly, carry the flowers well above the leaves on strong stems and are among the hardiest of the tropical kinds. They must still be considered as annuals in all but the warmest climates. They are day-bloomers and flower steadily from the time they are planted until the first frost or until they go dormant in December. They keep well in the house after being cut and are delightfully fragrant. The flowers are smaller than those of the other tropicals but larger than those of the hardies. Grow them exactly as you would any other tropical.

The Unforgettable Indian Lotus

There is considerable confusion about the name lotus. Once you have seen the East Indian lotus (*Nelumbium nelumbo*), with its big round leaves held above the water like parasols and the great flowers up to a foot across carried above the foliage for a total height of 6 or 8 feet, you will never confuse this plant with any other. The seed pods are also unique. When the flower opens, the top of the pod can be seen with a pattern of holes like the top of a salt shaker. When the flower has gone, the dry, brown, tapered bowl-shaped pods remain standing starkly on the strong stems. You have probably seen the dry pods in florists' shops where they are sold for use in flower arrangements.

One of the plants in the water lily genus (and one of the reasons for the confusion in the name) is *Nymphaea lotus*. The common name for this tropical lily is "white lotus of Egypt" or "sacred lily of the Nile." It is a lovely plant revered by the ancient Egyptians, but it is a water lily and not the stately lotus with which we are concerned here. The lotus motif that is so often seen in Egyptian and Oriental art is more likely to be based on this flower than on the genus *Nelumbium*. The *Nymphaea lotus* is white shaded to pink and it blooms from evening until noon the following day. The true lotus *(Nelumbium)* comes in a variety of colors, including white, pink, yellow and red, and has flower buds as round as a Chinese lantern that open in the morning and close at night. There are both single and double forms, and all are notably fragrant.

The East Indian lotus with parasol-like foliage stands out clearly in the center of the picture. When in flower it reaches a height of six to eight feet.

For all its exotic appearance the lotus is almost as tough and adaptable as the hardy lilies. It will grow and come up year after year wherever the growing points can be kept at a temperature above freezing. The lotus will tolerate, indeed thrive on, more clay in the soil than any of the lilies. The soil can be as much as one-fourth heavy clay and the plant will do well.

The lotus is a vigorous grower and the roots send runners underground. Unless you want them to take over a good-sized area on their own, they should be grown in containers. Round containers are best because they force the probing roots to grow in circles. In a square box the root may head into a corner and, for lack of a place to go, stop growing. Angled cleats in the corners of a square or rectangular container will diminish this danger.

The plant container should be about 20 inches in diameter and a foot deep. Use heavy clay soil and mix two cups of fertilizer in the bottom 2 inches. Saturate the soil before planting, as is recommended for the lilies. Dig a shallow depression and carefully lay the oblong tuber in, with at least a half inch of the growing tip clearly showing above the surface of the soil. This is important, because, if you cover the tips, the plant may fail. The roots may be brittle, so handle with care. Put about an inch of soil over them and do not touch the growing points. Add the inch of sand over the surface as recommended for all underwater plantings. The lotus has the same requirements for full sun as the lilies and does best where there are 4 to 6 inches of water above the level of the soil.

The plants may not flower the first year, but they will begin flowering the second season and will give you a good six months of bloom year after year as long as the growing points are protected from frost.

Lotus rooted in the bottom of a shallow pond

require no care except to be thinned out if they spread too far. If you have the patience for a little underwater work, plant the lotus in containers, to keep the roots from spreading, and embed the containers in the bottom of the pond. Put them where there will be 4 to 6 inches of water above the soil. Plastic tubs are best, because they will not disintegrate and let the plants escape.

Where there is danger of frost, the overwintering is rather more demanding than for the hardy lilies. When the plants go dormant in the fall and the foliage dies down, put the containers in a cool airy place where the temperature will go no lower than 35° or 40° F. If there is danger of attack by rats and mice, cover the soil with hardware cloth or other sturdy small-mesh screen. Keep the soil moist, but not saturated, throughout the winter. To keep the container-grown plants doing well, as with the hardy lilies, they should be lifted and divided and the soil replenished every two years. Lift the rootstock in the spring and cut a healthy section with a couple of growing points and replant as you did originally.

Lotus can be grown in 20-inch tubs on a terrace where they will make a marvelously dramatic display. Fill the container with soil to about 6 inches from the top and keep it brim full of water all through the growing season. A few small goldfish will add a glint of color and prevent mosquitoes from breeding in the water. Some growers feature lotus varieties that are somewhat smaller than usual and are recommended for growing above the ground in containers. You will find them in the catalogs.

How to Feed Lilies and Lotus

If you have mixed enough fertilizer into the bottom 2 inches of soil when the roots were planted, supplementary feeding should not be necessary. The indications of fertilizer depletion are smaller leaves of a yellow-green color and fewer flowers, of smaller size. A good side-dressing of fertilizer will produce quick and effective results when these symptoms appear.

Put a handful of plant food in a small paper sack and push it well into the soil alongside or under the roots. Unless you have access to the well-rotted manure that is considered to be the best water lily food, use the kind recommended by the grower from whom you bought the plants. Some dealers also have tablets of compressed fertilizer that are easily inserted and release plant food as they dissolve.

Any commercial fertilizer with an analysis of 10-10-10 will give good results. The numbers, in case you have forgotten, stand for percentages of nitrogen, phosphorus and potassium.

Coping with the Bugs and Blights

One of the joys of growing aquatic plants is their relative freedom from pests and disease. The most common invaders are the aphids that come to suck out the juices in the leaves. They can usually be washed away with a good strong spray of water. If you have a man-made pool and water lost by evaporation is not replaced by the rain, you must replenish it from time to time to maintain the level. Make it a habit to wash the leaves thoroughly whenever you add water whether you see any bugs or not. If the marauders persist, you can lay a section of hardware cloth over an area of lilies and weigh it down with rocks, to sink the foliage for a few hours. The leaves will survive the dunking but the aphids will not.

Most of the catalogs offer a spray for control of aphids. If used according to directions it will not harm the plants or fish.

Sometimes, but fortunately not often, you may see evidence of a fungus disease on the foliage. The recommended control is a fine spray of Bordeaux mixture on the foliage every other day for a week or more. Bordeaux is a mixture of copper sulphate and lime dissolved in water. Prepared forms are available in some garden stores. If not available, ask for an equivalent fungicide and use as directed. The most direct fungus control is to pick the infected leaves as soon as they appear, and get rid of them. Do not put diseased material in a compost pile. Burning, if legal in your area, is best.

If beetles, leaf miners, leaf-rollers or other obvious troublemakers are seen, pick them off and destroy them immediately.

Goldfish are the best pest control for the water garden. They are inexpensive, attractive and constantly feeding on a number of potential troublemakers. See Part III, Chapter 2.

4

Connoisseurs' Collection of Lilies and Lotus

There are hundreds more fine varieties of flowering aquatics available than even the most enthusiastic water gardener could grow in a back-yard pond or pool. The challenge is to decide which few will give you the most pleasurable return for your investment in time, space and money.

If the pool is at a distance from the terrace, or regularly seen from a window in the house, you may want to choose plants that stand up above the surface so that you can see the brilliance of their color at a distance. Of course, the lotus, with its flowers standing 6 feet high, is an ideal choice for a pool that is usually viewed from some distance. This is not to say that the entire pool should be given over to the lotus but it is a plant to be considered.

On the other hand, a pool adjacent to a sitting area or beside a much-used path or walkway suggests the planting of floating lilies that emphasize the flat place of water. Do not choose the plants until you have considered which heights and forms will give you the greatest reward.

If the pool is within easy view during the day, you will want some day-blooming kinds. All the hardy lilies and some of the tropicals are day-bloomers. Most of the day-blooming tropicals are fragrant and, if the pool is near a sitting area, this is a pleasant factor to consider. The night-blooming tropicals are in flower in time for dinner on the terrace and, with lights on them, are certain show-stoppers for an outdoor party.

There are various other subtleties of planning for their use but the point is to consider the setting and the situation and choose the plants that will provide the most pleasure. Most people consider color more important than form. The following lists are grouped by color and listed in alphabetical order. Keep in mind that if you want blue, only the tropicals have it; and if you want the changing bronzy colors, both the hardy and day-blooming tropical "changeables" or "autumn shades" have this characteristic. Names differ slightly from catalog to catalog, but they are near enough alike to avoid confusion.

Hardy Lilies, by Color

WHITE

Candida. A good clean white with upright bloom.

Dawn. Large rounded flower, fragrant.

Gladstone. Exceptionally large for a hardy lily.

Gonnere. A superb glistening white. Double flowers.

Hermine. Star-shaped flowers held upright.

Marliac albida. White petals, sepals flushed pink. Has the added advantage of fragrance. .

Odorata alba. Has good light green foliage and many small fragrant flowers.

Tuberosa richardsoni. Rounded flowers tinted a soft green. Has an exceptionally long season of bloom.

Virginale (or virginalis). Very large, pure white.

Chromatella. Good-sized, cup-shaped flowers of clear canary yellow. Mottled foliage.

Moorei. Has varicolored foliage and flowers a deep shade of yellow.

Sulphurea. Sulphur-yellow flowers, mottled foliage.

Sulphurea grandiflora. Much the same as the above. Flowers are borne well above the leaves.

Sunrise. Flowers a good clear color with unusual textured petals. Olive and maroon foliage.

PINK

There are many more hardy pinks to choose from than any other color. Here are a dozen fine ones.

Amabiles. Good-sized flower that changes shades of pink as it develops.

Formosa. Prolific bloom. Clear pink color.

Lustrous. Rose-pink with a silvery sheen. Another fine free bloomer.

Marguerite La Place. Color changes from rose-pink shading to soft lilac.

Marliac rosea. Attractive cup-shaped flower suffused with a lovely soft pink.

Masaniello. Another variegated variety with colors pink to carmine-red. Fragrant.

Mme. J. Chifflot. Exceptionally large flowers of an unusual glowing pink.

Pink Opal. Glowing deep pink petals with rounded ends. Flower stands above water. Good for cutting.

Pink Sensation. Free-blooming with clear solid color. Early to open, late to close. Fragrant.

Rene Gerard. Deep rose, variegated with darker shades of red.

Rose Arey. Star-shaped flower with pointed incurved petals. Bright color. Fragrant.

Sumptuosa. Fully double. Light rosy pink color deepening toward the center.

RED

While few in number, there is considerable variation in form and shades of color.

Attraction. Exceptionally large flower for a hardy. Up to 10 inches across. Color is garnet to dark red with yellow-tipped stamens.

Conqueror. Also a large flower but lighter red than Attraction. Has similar showy yellow-tipped stamens.

Escarboucle. Brilliant red petals. Garnet stamens.

Gloriosa. Early and long-blooming. Has smaller foliage and requires less space. Fragrant.

James Brydon. Broad curving petals. Rosy crimson color.

Newton. A showy star-burst of narrow pointed petals.

Picciola. Deep crimson flower held well above the water. Interesting mottled foliage.

Sultan. The nearest to a cherry-red. A dependable plant that blooms freely.

CHANGEABLES, SUNSET or AUTUMN SHADES

These are the hardy lilies in the red to yellow range that change color as they open and close on succeeding days. Here are a half dozen of the most readily available.

Aurora. Yellow to orange to dark red. Not large, good for a tub or small pool.

Chrysantha. Yellow, slowly changing to vermilion. Also a good size for smaller pools.

Comanche. Rosy pink with soft yellow overtones. Turns to a coppery bronze. Dependable bloomer. Can tolerate a little shade.

Indiana. Mostly red changing from orange tones to shades of copper. Blooms freely.

Robinsonii. Star-shaped flower. Color ranges from shades of red to shades of yellow. Requires full sun and shallower water than usual for hardy lilies.

Sioux. Opens yellow-bronze, and changes to copper-orange.

MINIATURES

These are delightful novelties to grow in a watertight tub on a terrace, or as an accent in a small pool. Some growers offer collections. Here are ten of the best hardies: White, White Laydekeri and White Pygmy. Yellow, *Pygmea hel-*

vola and Yellow Pygmy. Pink, Joanne Pring and Pink Laydekeri. Red, *Laydekeri fulgens* and Patricia. Changeable, *Fulva laydekeri* and Aurora. And, for good measure, three day-blooming tropicals: Violet, Colorato. Lavender, Dauben. Purple, Royal Purple.

Combine some of these, which open in the morning and close at dusk, with the night-blooming kinds from the list that follows and you can have 24 hours of bloom in your lily pond from spring until fall. These are the only water lilies that produce flowers of lavender, purple and blue. All of these tropicals are fragrant.

**Day-blooming
Tropicals by Color**

PURPLE

August Koch. Large flowers about the color of the violet-blue wisteria.

Blue Beauty. Color ranges from lilac to blue.

Mrs. Martin E. Randig. Dark purple-blue. Vigorous grower.

Royal Purple. Lilac-purple. Contrasting yellow sepals are attractive.

BLUE

Director Moore. Deep, almost navy blue flower.

Jupiter. Good rich blue. Long season of bloom.

Margaret Randig. Broad petals of rich blue.

Midnight. Dark violet to blue. Double flower.

Alice Tricker. Broad petals on a vigorous plant.

Mrs. George H. Pring. Exceptionally large, very fragrant and white as snow. A classic lily.

Ted Uber. Pure white with yellow stamens.

White Gigantea. Flowers are not large but they close only the first night, then stay open.

YELLOW

Aviator Pring. Large cup-shaped flower, rich yellow color and lots of bloom.

St. Louis. A large yellow star-shaped flower. The foliage is attractively mottled.

Yellow Dazzler. Chrome-yellow flower more flat than cup-shaped. A prolific bloomer.

Sunbeam. Clean clear yellow, as the name implies.

PINK to RED

Cleveland. Rose-pink with interesting mottled leaves.

General Pershing. Large double orchid pink. Exceptionally fragrant and long-blooming.

Mrs. C. W. Ward. Rosy pink. Good size, strong growth.

Pink Pearl. Good-sized silvery pink flower. Excellent for cutting.

Pink Platter. Long narrow petals make a flat, star-shaped flower.

Red Star. A deep rose, star-shaped flower.

CHANGEABLES or AUTUMN SHADES

Afterglow. Pink flower changing to rose.

General MacArthur. In the yellow-to-pink range.

Golden West. Peach pink turning to peach yellow.

Talisman. Has subtle changing shades of yellow-pink for an interesting effect.

**Lotus—The Most
Dramatic Plants in
the Water Garden**

WHITE

Juno. Clean white petals open flat. The showy stamens are a good shade of yellow.

Missouri. A partially double flower with petals that are somewhat textured.

Sir Galahad. Large flowers of purest white stand well above the water.

PINK to RED

Bisset. Wide petals of a good clear pink.

C. E. Hutchings. Bright red, cup-shaped flower with an interesting dark "eye" of stamens in the center.

Mr. George C. Hitchcock. Very large, rather star-shaped flowers in a good rosy shade of pink.

Emily G. Hutchings. Large, well-formed flowers of brightest pink. Shows up well under artificial light.

*Water lilies are as much
at home in a dooryard
garden as in a pond at a
place in the country.
They are available in
sizes that adapt them to
almost any garden
requirement.*

H. C. Haarstick. Very large for a night-bloomer. Bright red with bronzy-red leaves.

Omoran. Big rosy pink flowers with showy stamens of interesting orange-red.

Red Flare. A good bright red flower on a sturdy free-blooming plant.

WHITE

Album Grandiflorum. Lovely flowers of purest white.

Shiroman. Creamy double flowers turn white shortly after they open.

YELLOW

Flavescens. Soft yellow rounded flowers generously displayed on a free-blooming plant.

Luteum. This is another strong bloomer.

PINK

Kinshirin. Pink flowers softly flushed with white.

Speciosum. Dark rose-colored rounded flowers.

RED

Osiris. Large flowers of a good carmine-red.

Pekinese Rubrum. Rich red flowers, very large leaves.

Roseum Plenum. Red-to-pink fully double flowers.

Part III

OF STONE FROGS AND FISH

From the beginning stone has been part of a garden; at first because it was there and no one took the time to remove it. Then a gardener in ancient times—probably in China—sensed a relationship of stones to the surrounding plants and selected specimens of each to supplement the other.

In our gardens today the great sculptural rocks and boulders are seemingly a firm and permanent foundation. The fragility of the surrounding trees and shrubs and flowers is poignantly accentuated by the contrast.

The irony, and part of the greater beauty, of this relationship is that the seeds of the plants and the progeny of the fish and other living things will continue to reproduce and their offspring will still be growing when the stone has been worn down to sand and disappeared completely.

The gardener, in his wisdom, can still combine them as he wishes.

1
Using Rock and Stone to Best Advantage

The admitted masters of combining large stones with smaller rocks and pebbles to beguiling effect in their gardens are the Japanese. The concept of the pleasure garden they may have obtained from the Chinese, but they adapted it to their own needs and the smaller scale of their country and their gardens. The Oriental's feeling for the character of stone is beyond the understanding of most Occidentals. There are famous stones in Japan with names, and there are descriptive names for every kind and shape that can be imagined. A Japanese garden without stone is unthinkable, and the Japanese go to incredible lengths to achieve a desired effect.

An American landscape architect once visited gardens in Japan guided by a fellow designer from Tokyo. In one garden he was impressed by the great sense of repose and power expressed by a large stone. The owner of the garden thanked him for complimenting his favorite object. Only later did the American learn that this was a famous stone brought from a great distance and that two-thirds of its bulk was buried in the ground. The power of the total stone was somehow expressed in the third that was exposed. This concept is rather different from finding a few nice rocks and putting them around for a "Japanese effect."

In working with stone and rock in our own gardens we should develop our own aesthetic approach and sense of values and leave the Japanese point of view to the Japanese. The dry river made of sand or small pebbles to simulate a larger waterway—or the Sea of Japan—with larger stones for islands is particularly difficult to do well. From the poor copies usually seen in this country such an attempt is also better left alone, no matter how easy it may appear.

One of the most satisfying ways to choose rocks for an American garden is to regard them as pieces of natural sculpture. If you like the texture, color and form, you like the rock, and it can give you pleasure to have it in your garden where all its subtle forms and colors can be revealed in the changing light of day and in all kinds of weather through the seasons. Such rocks are not easy to find and, if large enough to make much of an impact, not easy to get into the garden once you have found them. This is not to say that the search is not worth while. When a rock is found that can make a significant contribution to the garden scene—as would a piece of sculpture—it must be effectively displayed.

Using Stone as Sculpture

With or without the addition of water, stones can be strong sculptural elements in a garden scene. Possible combinations of shape, size and texture are endlessly challenging.

It is better to underplay than to overplay it. If it is set discreetly at the edge of a shrub border, in a setting of trees or combined with a planting of low-growing evergreens, there will be some pleasure of discovery when it is seen. What you should not do is put it in the middle of the lawn.

If you do not find a single stone worthy of setting up as a piece of sculpture, look for a few that can be grouped together to make a handsome showing. Pieces less than sculpture-size can be effectively displayed as islands in a pool or pond, mostly submerged, with the top breaking the surface of the water. Raked gravel or sand is an appropriate base for a display of stone. They are essentially the same material and the flat monochromatic surface is a good foil for the rugged irregularity of the chosen stone.

The Virtues of Gravel

For interesting texture, low cost and ease of upkeep a ground cover of gravel is excellent. It is so appealing that it is often used in areas larger than they should be. Too much gravel can seem barren and uninviting. It is at its best in reasonably small areas as a contrast to a lawn or other surface cover.

In a small concrete decorative pool it is most attractive spread evenly over the bottom. The water accentuates the color, of which there is considerable in some gravels, and the silt that is sure to settle in a pool disappears neatly between the pieces. It is a natural to use for the bed of any stream or pond.

As a cover in a planting of succulents or cactus, gravel is ideal; and wherever water drops, (as from a faulty downspout or from the eaves), a well-placed strip of gravel will eliminate splash and spatter.

Rounded river-washed rock has an appeal all its own and it is the kind of useful souvenir one can bring back from almost any trip. A collection of such rocks, symmetrical and reasonably uniform in size, can be used for a cobblestone effect in small areas too narrow for growing grass or other ground covers—often the case between a house or garage and a parallel service walk. A flat tray filled with selected rocks and placed under a faucet provides a pleasant glistening accent. Or a frame of 2 by 2's can be made to fit around the rocks as a frame around a picture.

The framing idea can also be used with raked gravel. Make a rectangular border with 2 by 4's and fill the area inside with gravel. This makes a flat stage upon which you can display a piece of garden sculpture, a large sculptural rock, or a dramatic piece of driftwood. Here, again, the matter of relative scale becomes particularly important. The gravel rectangle should be the right size in relation to its immediate surroundings, and the pieces displayed should be in proper scale with the panel on which they sit. Remember the marginal sketches on page 45? "Good scale" means that something is neither too large nor too small for its setting.

Cherish the Rock You Have

If you are fortunate enough to have an outcropping of rock on your property, do everything you can to dramatize it and show it at its best. The best of all possible rock gardens are made by planting in cracks and crevices and a few man-made pockets in a natural showing of rock. If the top of a rock shows through the earth you can probe with an iron rod and see where it goes. If it doesn't drop away too steeply, perhaps you can remove the overlying soil and find that you have one of nature's greatest gifts—a ready-made piece of the earth's crust.

The Oriental Approach

Any one of the many elegant effects seen here could be used to enhance a small pool: the bridge, the stone lantern, river-washed rocks, or the well-shaped stones and plants.

Very little water can be effective in a garden setting, especially if the container is interesting in its own right.

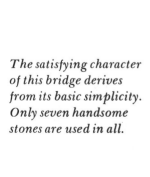

The satisfying character of this bridge derives from its basic simplicity. Only seven handsome stones are used in all.

*Plants can be selected
and pruned to reveal
their best aspects against
a plain background of
water.*

*The forms of the stones
at water's edge are subtly
echoed in the shape of
the surrounding plants.*

2

Fish, Frogs and Other Visitors

Frogs, turtles and often some fish will appear on the scene in a large pond in the country. Even a suburban lily pond will usually attract a few welcome amphibians. A farm pond can be stocked with fish, and your County Agent will give you complete information as to the game fish that will flourish. Whether you should try bass, bluegills or bream is a matter too specialized to deal with here. To stock the backyard pond or pool requires some planning and a visit to the pet store or ordering from a catalog supplier.

Anyone with a small pool the size of a laundry tub or larger can keep fish the year round outdoors. As explained earlier, fish are needed to balance the oxygen and carbon dioxide relationship in the pool and they are also efficient scavengers that will help keep the pool clear of insects and their larvae and eggs. Not the least of their useful service is the virtual elimination of the breeding of mosquitoes in the pool.

The hardiest and among the most attractive fish to have in an outdoor pool are the common goldfish. Their bright brassy color catches the sun and adds welcome life and movement to the placid waters.

Some fish-fanciers may consider the common variety too ordinary to deserve pool space but it is the hardiest of the lot and for all-round satisfaction is hard to beat. A few of these should certainly be included. While the unusual characteristics of the fantails, telescope celestials and lionheads are not so easy to see in an outdoor pool as in an aquarium, a few of them are worth having for contrast. A variety of fish adds interest.

Fish are now shipped in water-filled plastic bags, and a number of choices are offered by the mail-order dealers. Your local pet store will also have some to offer for the outdoor pool. The most popular kinds of hardy goldfish are the common, comet, calico fantail, Japanese fantail, moor and shubunkin.

The one you have brought home from the dime store in the classic glass bowl is the common. It has scales of shining gold and is a good strong swimmer. There are other colors, too—silvery, yellow-gold and mottled red and black.

The comet is a variety developed in America. It has long fins and tail which make it a faster swimmer than most of the other goldfish—which accounts for the name. Its pattern of darting movement is an interesting contrast to the motion of the other fish. The color is essentially the same as that of the common goldfish.

Japanese fantail. The double fins and long graceful double tail give this fish its name. It is a slow, stately swimmer which makes it easy to see and inspect.

Calico fantail. This is one of the so-called scaleless fish. They do have scales but they are transparent and the fish has a smooth texture that seems to glow in the light. The smooth texture clearly reveals the bright, mottled colors. It also has the long fins and tail characteristic of the fantails.

Moor. A small black fish of elegant proportions. Its primary attraction is its complete difference in color from all the other fish. It is much easier to see in an aquarium than in a pool.

Shubunkin. Introduced in the early 1900's, this is one of the more recent developments in hybrid goldfish. It is also of the scaleless type and boasts a subtle blending of colors. No two are alike, which makes them favorites of collectors.

Care and Feeding

The first consideration is to make sure you do not have more fish in the pool than it can support. The available oxygen is the limiting factor. The usual formula for determining how many fish your pool will accommodate is to allow at least 20 square inches of water surface for each inch of fish. Fish that you buy are sized by the inch; the measurement does not include the tail. Let us consider, for example, how many fish can live happily in a pool that measures 4 by 5 feet. This area totals about 2900 square inches of surface. Divide this by 20 (square inches per fish) and we find that the pool can handle 140 inches. This would be 20 7-inchers, except that these will grow, and it would be better to think in terms of 14 smaller fish that may get to be 10 inches when they are mature.

Don't Kill Them with Kindness

More goldfish are killed by being overfed than by any other cause. In the natural state they had to forage for themselves. Although raised for generations in captivity they have not lost the knack. They are still able to seek out and survive on all kinds of bits and pieces in the pool, which also helps to keep the water clean. If you overfeed them they will not concentrate on scavenging and, worse yet, the food they can't eat will break down and cloud the water.

Never put in more food than the fish can eat in five minutes. And if they miss a few meals during the week it will do them more good than harm. The best food to use is that which is sold by the dealer from whom you got the fish. It is probably what they were raised on.

The major pool cleaning should probably be

done in the spring when the water lilies are renewed and replanted, and when you want it to be at its best for early-season outdoor living. There should also be a careful cleanup in the winter if any leaves have fallen into the water. They will decompose over the winter and give off noxious gasses that can harm the overwintering fish—even if they are in a state of near-hibernation. Oak and maple leaves are particularly toxic and should definitely be removed.

When it is time for the spring cleanup, net the fish out gently and put them into a large container of the water in which they have been living. Fill the pool with a fine spray from the hose. The spray will help oxygenate the new supply of water. Let the water adjust to the temperature of the pool and the air and release some of its impurities, such as chlorine, for a couple of days before replacing the fish. Do not throw them back in. They are not as tough as you might think. Sink the container in which they were stored into the pool and let them swim out.

New fish are introduced to the pool in much the same way. The water-filled plastic bags in which the fish come should be floated in the pool water long enough to equalize the temperature between the two. The point is to avoid the shock of quick temperature change. When the adjustment is made, slit the bag and let the fish out.

Putting Fish in a New Pool

A new pool of concrete, concrete block or brick will give off unhealthy chemicals for some time after it is filled. These will dissipate into the water and into the air, but it takes time. The new pool should be filled and allowed to adjust itself for a few weeks before fish are put in. Plants can, and should, be put in first. They will help to introduce more oxygen and will do a little clarifying and purifying of the water themselves.

The hardy goldfish, including all those mentioned above, will make it nicely through the winter under ice if there is a foot or so of unfrozen water for them to float in. They need no food during this time, and there will be enough oxygen in the water to keep them alive. As mentioned before it is a good idea to put a piece of wood or ball in the water and push it gently from time to time to keep an opening to admit more oxygen and to reduce the pressure of the ice on the sides of the pool.

There are various snails that spend their lives feeding on the algae and other unsightly particles in a pool. They are a welcome addition and are available from pool supply dealers. Tadpoles also eat algae and decaying matter, and they have the added advantage of turning into frogs which help to keep the insects from getting out of control.

Thus it is, even at the minute size of the tadpoles and algae, that balances are established in nature. They develop in pond and puddle. They occur in the soil itself and among the flowers, birds and bees. The subtle relationships of natural balance are fundamental to all life and are at the root of the eternal fascination that planting and growing a garden holds for all of us.

The charm of color and movement in a pool can easily be attained by adding decorative fish.

Suggested Catalogs

Paradise Gardens. 14 May St. Whitman, Mass. 02382

They offer a wide variety of plastic pools and pool liners, pumps and spray heads. They also carry water lilies, other aquatic plants and fish.

Three Springs Fisheries. Lilypons, Maryland. 21717

Here you will find a large selection of water lilies of all types as well as lotus and many other aquatic plants. Their extensive goldfish collection is shown in color photographs.

William Tricker.
174 Allendale Ave. Saddle River, N.J. 07458
7125 Tanglewood Drive, Independence, Ohio. 44131

The catalog includes many kinds of water lilies. Lotus and other aquatics are listed as well as fish. Collections sold in groups are featured.

Van Ness Water Gardens.
2460 N. Euclid Ave. (Crescent West),
Upland, Calif. 91786

Here is a complete range of lilies and other aquatic plants, including water iris. Pumps, spray heads, pool liners and lights are also shown.

Pumps, Fountains,
Pools and Lights

Little Giant Pump Co.
3810 N. Tulsa St. Oklahoma City, Oklahoma 73112

Rain Jet Corp.
301 South Flower St. Burbank, Calif. 91503

Index

Plant Hardiness Zone Map

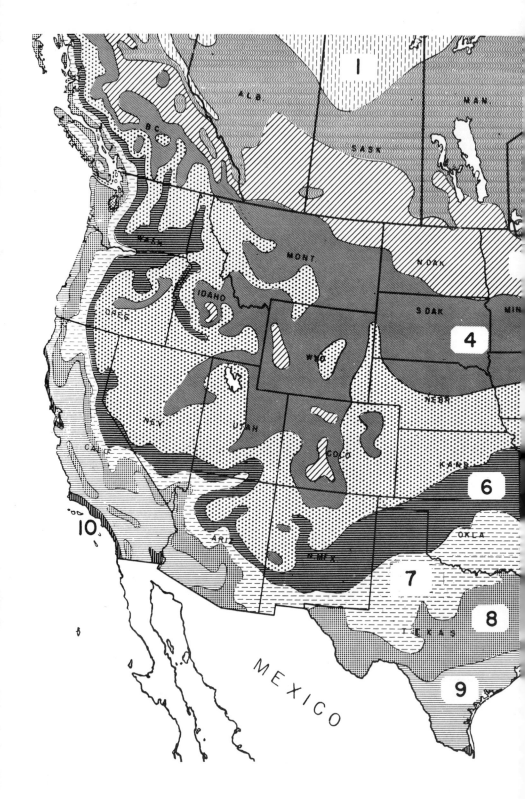

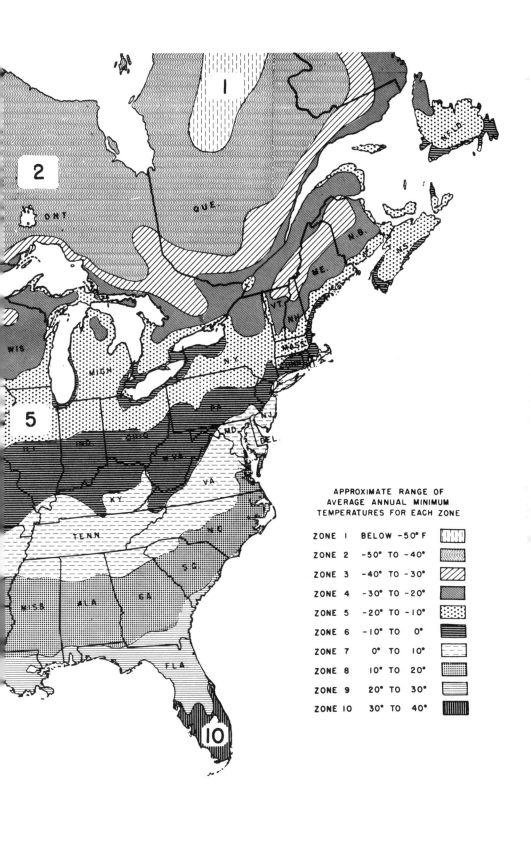

APPROXIMATE RANGE OF
AVERAGE ANNUAL MINIMUM
TEMPERATURES FOR EACH ZONE

ZONE 1   BELOW −50° F

ZONE 2   −50° TO −40°

ZONE 3   −40° TO −30°

ZONE 4   −30° TO −20°

ZONE 5   −20° TO −10°

ZONE 6   −10° TO   0°

ZONE 7   0° TO 10°

ZONE 8   10° TO 20°

ZONE 9   20° TO 30°

ZONE 10   30° TO 40°